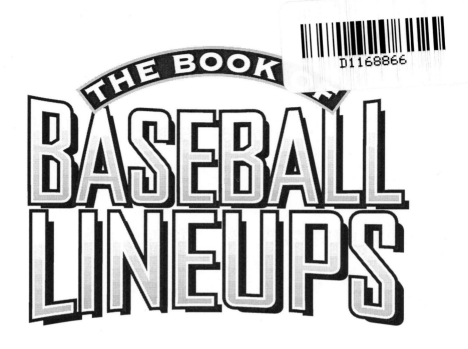

THE BOOK OF BASEBALL LINEUPS

NICHOLAS ACOCELLA AND DONALD DEWEY

A CITADEL PRESS BOOK
Published by Carol Publishing Group

For Bart Acocella, for being there all the time
And Allen Ryan, for all his support

A Citadel Press Book
Published by Carol Publishing Group
Citadel Press is a registered trademark of Carol Communications, Inc.
Editorial Offices: 600 Madison Avenue, New York, N.Y. 10022
Sales and Distribution Offices: 120 Enterprise Avenue, Secaucus, N.J. 07094
In Canada: Canadian Manda Group, One Atlantic Avenue, Suite 105, Toronto,
    Ontario M6K 3E7
Queries regarding rights and permissions should be addressed to Carol
Publishing Group, 600 Madison Avenue, New York, N.Y. 10022

Carol Publishing Group books are available at special discounts for bulk
purchases, sales promotion, fund-raising, or educational purposes. Special
editions can be created to specifications. For details, contact: Special Sales
Department, Carol Publishing Group, 120 Enterprise Avenue,
Secaucus, N.J. 07094

Manufactured in the United States of America
10   9   8   7   6   5   4   3   2   1

Library of Congress Cataloging-in-Publication Data
Acocella, Nick.
    The book of baseball lineups / Nicholas Acocella and Donald Dewey.
       p.   cm.
    "A Citadel Press book."
    ISBN 0–8065–1753–0 (pbk.)
    1. Baseball—Anecdotes   2. Baseball—Miscellanea.   I. Dewey,
Donald, 1940–   .   II. Title.
GV873.A36   1996
796.357—dc20   95–47104
                                                        CIP

CONTENTS

CONTENTS

PREFACE

Baseball fans thrive on statistics, conjecture, and argument. A fan who doesn't know that Ted Williams reached base in 17 consecutive at-bats or that Joe DiMaggio hit in 56 consecutive games is someone who goes to the refreshment stand for a hot dog when the home team has loaded the bases in the bottom of the ninth. A fan who doesn't wonder about what might have happened if the Red Sox had held on to Babe Ruth or if Mickey Mantle hadn't gotten hurt in 1961 has no imagination. One who has no opinion about Pete Rose's Cooperstown credentials is better off playing computer games. Baseball is numbers, fantasy, and creed, and the baseball fan is someone who spends each season, hot-stove league, and spring training trying to marshal these elements into an explanation for what actually happens on the field. The uninformed call it a pastime; the true fan knows there is little leisure involved.

The Book of Baseball Lineups is a compendium of statistics, conjecture, and argument. Its format—the lineup—is not only baseball's most basic organizational unit but also the scheme most commonly adopted by millions of fans when they muse about the best and the worst, the greatest and the most grating, the most overrated and the most underrated. Included, of course, are lineups that point up the achievements of the Cobbs and the Robinsons, but also included are those that illustrate the uniqueness of the Chapmans and the Niemans. On the following pages, the Joosts become the teammates of the Mathewsons, the Cuccinellos of the Yastrzemskis, the Sparky Andersons of the Gair Allies—and all for usually overlooked reasons.

In general, there are three kinds of lineups in this book. The first group consists of teams put together on the basis of cold numbers. Many players may have seemed great at this or that, but what exactly do the statistical facts say? Included in this group are such lineups as the best hitters in the history of the game (none of whom is in the Hall of Fame), the worst hitters of all time (none of whom ever got a hit), and one of the strangest collections of all: players who held down starting berths for one season but otherwise never wore a big league uniform.

A second group of lineups concerns the identical, the coincidental, and the bizarre: a hurler who arrived on the scene to pitch a no-hitter and then disappeared; a catcher carried on a roster just to instigate fights; a team of players blacklisted from organized baseball. Not to mention lineups that present the familiar in unfamiliar terms—for example, a team of players who ended the most noted pitching streaks. They're all here.

Last, but hardly least, are the lineups of the purest prejudice—those in which the authors expose themselves to criticism for their perhaps foolish opinions. Our only defense for the selections in this group is that of age: We never asked Cap Anson for his autograph, never saw Chuck Klein hit a ball into the bleachers. But it is also in these lineups that *The Book of Baseball Lineups* has its primary purpose—to start an argument.

Nicholas Acocella
Donald Dewey

AUTHORS' NOTE

For the sake of clarity, we refer throughout the book to existing major league franchises by their present nicknames; here, for example, the Yankees are always the Yankees, even though they were once the Highlanders. Extinct clubs, such as the various National League (NL) Washington franchises of the last century, are referred to by their cities. Teams in third major leagues, such as the Players League (PL), are identified by city and league.

The lineup is essentially an instrument of offense. However, for almost all the teams based on cold numbers, we have selected a pitcher who was good at preventing what the hitters on the same page did so well; in one, there is a designated hitter (in others a pitcher) whose offensive accomplishments are consistent with those of the position players.

All statistics, and the opinions based on them, run only through the 1995 season. All statistics through the 1992 season come from the revised ninth edition of *The Baseball Encyclopedia;* the source for the last three years is the official totals of the two major leagues.

MOST INFLUENTIAL—ON THE FIELD

Those earning recognition here were either innovative in their approach or daring in their skills, but when all the members of this team hung up their spikes, the sport was significantly different from the one they had known as rookies.

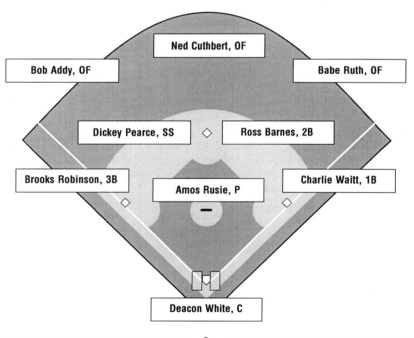

Waitt was the first player to wear a glove on the field, an innovation he adopted for St. Louis of the proto–major league National Association in 1875. Take away Waitt's skintight glove, which, with cut-off fingers, looked more appropriate for lifting weights than for handling throws from other infielders, and you would have to erase everything from Walter Johnson's victories and Nolan Ryan's no-hitters to a mean batting average of .250. He later went on to a modest three-year major league career in the 1870s and 1880s as an outfielder.

BABE RUTH
NEW YORK YANKEES – OUTFIELD   1927

Babe Ruth reinvented the game with his long-ball hitting.

The first major league superstar, Barnes batted .429 (63 points higher than the runner-up) in the NL's inaugural season of 1876. The following year, his specialty—the fair-foul hit, a batted ball that bounced fair then squiggled foul before reaching a fielder—was declared a foul ball. Had Barnes not been so proficient at this ploy, modern hitters might have made more of an effort to drive the ball into the dirt in front of them instead of over the fences. Barnes's troubles in 1877 didn't end with the Rules Committee; he also suffered a muscular disorder that kept him out of the lineup for more than half of Chicago's games and helped lower his batting average to .272.

Robinson's fancy glove work forever altered baseball's attitude toward third base. Before Brooks, the hot corner was, as often as not, a place to hide a slugger with a strong chest and little else in the way of defensive skills.

Pearce, who played in only 33 major league games, for the St. Louis NL franchise in 1876 and 1877, influenced the game forever with his innovation (in the 1850s) of moving in from an original softball-like short-field position to the infield spot where shortstops from Honus Wagner to Cal Ripken have left their marks. He has also been credited with inventing both the bunt (or "tricky hit," as it was called in his day) and the fair-foul hit (Barnes's specialty). In the NL's inaugural year, he also started the first triple play in the major leagues.

Addy is generally regarded as the first player to slide into a base. Later an outfielder with the Cubs (1876) and Reds (1877), he pioneered the technique while playing for the Forest City club of Rockford, Illinois, in 1866.

Cuthbert didn't even wait for Addy's innovation. He stole third base in an 1865 game while playing for the Philadelphia Keystones against the astonished Brooklyn Atlantics. His explanation for the move was the best possible: There was no rule forbidding it. He later appeared in five major league seasons, at a time (the 1870s and 1880s) when stolen bases were not recorded.

Ruth's home runs, with their ability to draw crowds, so impressed major league owners that the lively ball was introduced in 1921. The result was an offensive explosion that redefined the game.

It was either White or contemporary Nat Hicks who was the first catcher to move up directly behind the plate, a position the Deacon assumed, as early as 1875, when there were runners on base. White was certainly the one who designed the first chest protector (in 1884), an inspiration that made such positioning a little less life threatening.

It was Rusie's dominance of NL hitters in the early 1890s (94 wins and almost 1,000 strikeouts between 1890 and 1892) that led baseball officialdom to increase the distance between the mound and home plate from fifty feet to sixty feet six inches. The righthander adjusted handily to the new dimensions: In the first three seasons after the change (1893–95), he won another 92 games, even though his strikeout total dropped to 604.

Honorable mention to players whose ingenuity dictated a change in the rules:

Phillies' outfielder Roy Thomas, whose penchant for standing up at the plate and fouling off pitches to his heart's content prompted the NL in 1901 to introduce a regulation declaring a batter's first two fouls strikes. (The American League [AL] would follow suit two years later.) Pitching strategy would never be the same again, nor would hitting .400 prove as easy.

Cincinnati third baseman Don Hoak, who grabbed a potential double-play grounder while running from second to third and casually tossed the ball to Milwaukee shortstop Johnny Logan. Under the rules in force at the time (1957), Hoak was called out, and the ball was declared dead, but he had accomplished his purpose in foiling the double play. Soon thereafter, a new regulation declared both runner and batter out in the event of deliberate interference with a batted ball by a base runner.

To those who changed the nature of baseball equipment: Fred Thayer, who was captain of the Harvard University nine when he designed the first catcher's mask in 1877; Providence (NL) shortstop Art Irwin, who designed the first padded mitt, in 1885, to protect two broken fingers; Cardinal pitcher Bill Doak, who, in 1920, sported the first glove with a preformed pocket and reinforced webbing; Detroit first baseman Hank Greenberg, whose attempt to employ an oversized mitt in 1938 led to restrictions on the dimensions of fielders' gloves; Pittsburgh slugger Ralph Kiner, who introduced the first batting helmet in the late 1940s; Kansas City outfielder Ken Harrelson, who, in 1964, was the first to wear batting gloves in a game; and catcher Randy Hundley of the Cubs, who, in the late 1960s, introduced the hinged flip-over mitt that made one-handed catching commonplace.

And to the hurlers who were unrelenting in their search for trick pitches to get batters out: Candy Cummings for inventing the curveball in the 1860s; Tricky Nichols for throwing the first sinker in 1875; Charlie Sweeney for coming up with the screwball in the 1880s; Toad Ramsey for discovering the effects of the knuckleball in the 1880s; Frank Corridon for popularizing the spitball in 1902; Dave Keefe for realizing in the 1910s that his missing middle finger made possible the fork ball; George Blaeholder for pioneering the slider in the 1920s; and Roger Craig for devising the split-finger fastball in the 1970s.

A special nod to James Creighton of the Brooklyn Excelsiors, who, in the late 1850s, discovered that by snapping his wrist at the conclusion of his underhand delivery, he added both speed and spin to the ball. That the innovation was illegal under the amateur rules of the day was largely ignored. Before Creighton, the relationship between batsman and pitcher more closely resembled that between a modern hitter and batting-practice pitcher; after Creighton, batters would never again feel as confident—or as safe.

MOST INFLUENTIAL—OFF THE FIELD

This lineup exists because boardroom and courtroom wrangles have been as crucial to the history of baseball as on-the-field heroics. For every player who made his impact with a bat or a glove, another left his mark with the assistance of a lawyer or an agent; still others were caught up in situations over which they had little control. But whether it was because of what they did or what was done to them, all the members of this team—no less than those included in the previous one—altered forever the game they played.

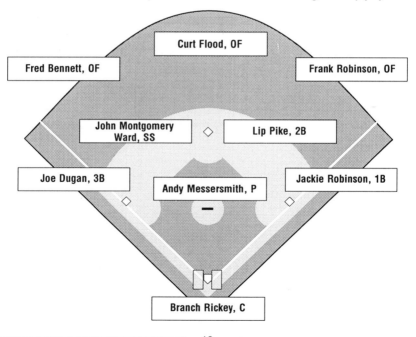

Curt Flood, OF

Fred Bennett, OF

Frank Robinson, OF

John Montgomery Ward, SS

Lip Pike, 2B

Joe Dugan, 3B

Andy Messersmith, P

Jackie Robinson, 1B

Branch Rickey, C

Robinson's major league debut in 1947 started the erosion of baseball's racial barriers and changed the racial composition of every future team.

While there is considerable argument as to the identity of the first player to be paid for his services, Pike had a major hand in exposing the hypocrisy of under-the-table remuneration of ostensible amateurs when he and two teammates refused to appear before a committee of the National Association of Base Ball Players to answer charges that they had accepted money from the Philadelphia Athletics in 1866. That their accusers also failed to show up for the hearing speaks eloquently to the question of just how seriously the amateur status of baseball was taken. Thereafter, money changed hands between owners and players openly.

Dugan's trade from the Red Sox to the Yankees in August 1922 helped the New Yorkers edge the St. Louis Browns for the AL pennant. When the Browns objected to the late season deal, Commissioner Kenesaw Mountain Landis imposed the June 15 trading deadline, which remained officially in effect until the 1980s.

After more than a century of existence, the reserve clause died when Andy Messersmith's grievance ushered in the free-agent era.

Ward was the president and guiding hand of the Players Brotherhood of the late 1880s that evolved into the PL of 1890, an effort to free players from the reserve clause. While the PL drew most of the stars of the day, it nevertheless collapsed after only one season. The players did, however, win several lawsuits on the central issue, most notably one leveled at Ward himself. After his playing career ended, lawyer Ward represented several players in actions against their teams.

Bennett's appeal to Landis, in 1930, that the Browns had buried him in the minor leagues after only 7 games with the parent club brought him free agency and an additional, however undistinguished, season in the majors. But it also brought Landis the only lawsuit of his tenure, filed by St. Louis owner Phil Ball. A federal judge decided in the commissioner's favor on the immediate issue of freeing Bennett, but of more widespread importance, he also strongly upheld the right of major league teams to maintain farm systems.

Flood's refusal to accept a trade from the Cardinals to the Phillies in 1969 led to the eventual elimination of the reserve clause. Although the U.S. Supreme Court decided against Flood in 1972, its decision invited a closer look at the special status of baseball, an invitation readily accepted by the Players Association just a few years later.

Frank Robinson was to managers what Jackie Robinson had been to players. He cracked the color line for dugout bosses when he was appointed player-manager of the Indians in 1975.

Rickey's most memorable moment as a backstop came when he allowed a record 13 stolen bases on June 28, 1907; as a front-office official, his record was somewhat more positive. For the Cardinals, he developed the farm system in the 1920s, eventually building a network that at its height claimed thirty-two affiliates; as president of the Dodgers, he picked Jackie Robinson to integrate baseball.

In 1975, Messersmith successfully challenged the reserve clause and paved the way for the free-agent era when he secured his freedom from the Los Angeles Dodgers through a grievance decided in his favor by arbitrator Peter Seitz.

Honorable mention to second baseman Lou Bierbauer, who, in the aftermath of the PL war of 1890, chose not to return to his old club, the American Association (AA) Philadelphia Athletics, but elected instead to sign with Pittsburgh of the NL. Relatively well known is that his new team became the Pirates forever after; less so is that his defection led to a new war between the two surviving circuits, one that destroyed the AA.

The hierarchy of the Most Influential franchise would include:

Umpire Alexander Cartwright, who drew up the first written rules of the game (establishing, among other things, nine men to a side and ninety feet between the bases) and who umpired what is traditionally considered the first game, at Elysian Fields in Hoboken, New Jersey, on June 19, 1846.

Entrepreneur William Cammeyer, who built the first enclosed ballpark, Union Grounds in Brooklyn, in 1862; his park enabled him to popularize the concept of charging admission to ball games.

Cincinnati civic booster Aaron Champion, who decided, in 1869, to create the first professional baseball team. The Red Stockings launched a fabled winning streak that went on for anywhere from 56 to 130 games (depending on the version of the story used) and thereby sowed the seeds of their own destruction: Shortly after the streak was snapped by the Brooklyn Atlantics in June 1870, the team disbanded because it couldn't afford the high salaries its players commanded.

Official scorer Henry Chadwick, who codified the rules of the National Pastime in the 1870s and was its first official scorer.

NL founder William Hulbert, who, in 1876, scuttled the player-controlled proto—major league National Association and, as owner of the Cubs, persuaded his peers to form the owner-dominated National League.

Owner Arthur Soden of the Braves, who introduced the reserve clause in 1879 and thus began more than a century of strife between players and management.

AL president Ban Johnson, who, in 1901, launched the only successful challenge to the NL's monopoly.

It is impossible to imagine either the business or mythology of baseball without Al Spalding, a nineteenth-century player, manager, and owner. Aside from his longtime association with both the Cubs and the company (bearing his name) that made sporting goods a thriving industry, he was also the driving force behind the 1905 commission that gave official sanction to the myth that baseball was the spontaneous creation of Abner Doubleday.

Inventor George Cahill, who demonstrated as early as 1909 the efficacy of a light tower that would make night baseball possible, even though it would be another twenty-six years before the first major league game was played under the lights.

And finally Oliver Wendell Holmes, who, as a member of the Supreme Court nine, wrote the 1922 decision granting baseball exemption from antitrust legislation.

HISTORIC FIRSTS

A relatively easy way of getting into the record book is to have been around for the first major league game. Six members of this team were on the field for that initial NL contest, between Boston and Philadelphia, on April 22, 1876. It took a few days or a few years for the others to accomplish their historic firsts.

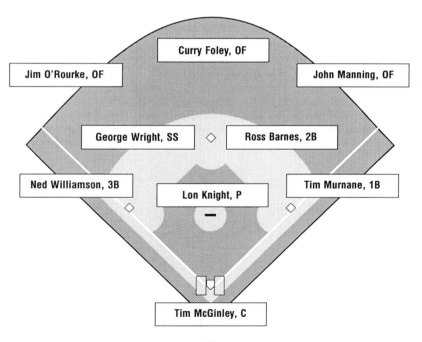

In Philadelphia, on April 22, 1876, Knight threw the first major league pitch.

The first batter was Boston's Wright, who made the very first out by grounding to short.

O'Rourke touched Knight for the first hit, a two-out single in the first inning.

McGinley scored the first run, for Boston.

Manning drove him in.

The Braves' Murnane stole the first base.

Ten days after the NL inaugural, the Cubs' Barnes became the first player to hit a home run.

On May 30, 1884, Chicago's Williamson went into the books as the first to sock 3 homers in a single contest.

Foley completed the major leagues' first cycle (knocking a single, a double, a triple, and a home run in the same game) on May 25, 1882, for Buffalo.

Knight's teammates chalked up a few firsts of their own in his 6–5 loss to Boston:

Third baseman Ezra Sutton threw wildly to first for the first error.

A veteran of the fabled 1869–70 Cincinnati Red Stockings, George Wright was the first batter in the major leagues.

Outfielder Dave Eggler caught a fly ball and threw a Boston runner out at the plate to complete the first double play.

And fellow outfielder Levi Meyerle was credited with the first double and the first base on balls. A few days later, Meyerle also legged out the first triple.

The first winning pitcher was Boston's Joe Borden.

Honorable mention to:

Troy's slugging first baseman Roger Connor, who hit the first grand slam, on September 10, 1881.

Charlie Reilly, an otherwise undistinguished third baseman, who stroked the first pinch hit, a ninth-inning single for the Phillies, on April 28, 1892.

And to Al Spalding of the Cubs, whose 4–0 blanking of Louisville, on April 25, 1876, was the first shutout.

HIGHEST CAREER BATTING AVERAGES

Hitting a baseball successfully is probably the most difficult feat in sports. Using a tapered, cylindrical stick of wood, a batter must redirect a sphere $2\frac{7}{8}$ inches in diameter thrown toward him at between 75 and 100 miles an hour in such a way that it might spin, dip, or curve out of his reach. He must hit the ball within a range of ninety degrees while having it elude nine opponents eager to stop it. Only in baseball, therefore, does failure two-thirds of the time amount to remarkable success. These players were the most successful over at least ten seasons in the twentieth century.

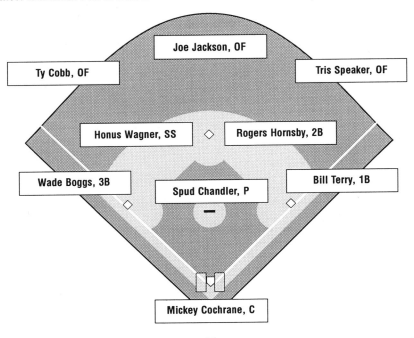

Joe Jackson, OF

Ty Cobb, OF

Tris Speaker, OF

Honus Wagner, SS

Rogers Hornsby, 2B

Wade Boggs, 3B

Spud Chandler, P

Bill Terry, 1B

Mickey Cochrane, C

Terry's .341 over fourteen years (1923–36) for the Giants edges out George Sisler and Lou Gehrig (both .340). Dave Orr hit .342, but he played only eight seasons (1883–90).

Hornsby's .358 average with five teams from 1915 to 1937 is the second highest in history.

Boggs's .334 in fourteen seasons (1982–95) with the Red Sox and Yankees is much higher than runner-up Pie Traynor's .320. Only John McGraw's .333 from 1891 to 1906 is closer to Boggs's average.

Most of Wagner's .327 average was compiled in the twentieth century; he played for Louisville and Pittsburgh from 1897 to 1917.

All-time leader Cobb hit .367 from 1905 to 1928 for the Tigers and Athletics.

Jackson's .356 is third on the all-time list. His career, with the Athletics, Indians, and White Sox from 1908 to 1920, ended because of his role in the Black Sox scandal.

Speaker, .345 from 1907 to 1928 for four AL clubs, gets the nod over Lefty O'Doul (.349), who was a pitcher for four of his eleven seasons. Ed Delahanty (.346) loses out because most of his career was in the last century.

JOE JACKSON
RIGHT FIELD
CHICAGO "WHITE SOX" A. L.

Joe Jackson has the highest average of any player without a Cooperstown plaque.

Cochrane's .320 average for the Athletics and Tigers from 1925 to 1937 is a full 7 points higher than second-place Bill Dickey's .313.

Chandler's 109–43 record for the Yankees between 1937 and 1947 gives him a .717 won-lost percentage, the highest for pitchers with at least 100 victories.

For a pitcher with 200 or more wins, there is Whitey Ford, 236–106 (.690) in seventeen years with the Yankees. Bob Caruthers's .692 (218–97) was better than Ford's, but his nine-year career ended in 1892.

The best won-lost percentage among managers with at least 1,000 games is Joe McCarthy's .615 (2,125 wins and 1,333 losses) for the Cubs, Yankees, and Red Sox in twenty-four seasons between 1926 and 1950.

Honorable mention to Babe Ruth, whose .304 average as a pitcher is the best ever; and to Tommy Davis, whose .320 (63-for-197) is the highest pinch-hitting average.

HIGHEST SEASON BATTING AVERAGES

The players in this lineup have the highest averages for a single year:

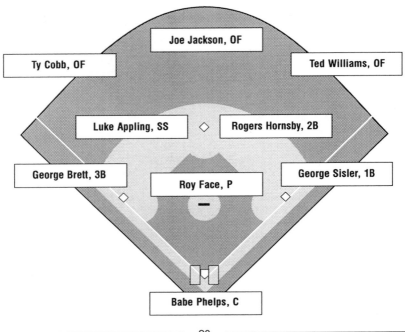

Sisler hit .420 for the St. Louis Browns in 1922.

Hornsby holds the twentieth-century record—.424 for the 1924 Cardinals.

Brett finished at .390 for the 1980 Royals.

Appling's .388 for the White Sox in 1936 is as high as any shortstop has ever hit.

The loftiest of Cobb's three .400 seasons was .420 for the 1911 Tigers.

Jackson batted .408 for the Indians in 1911.

The most recent .400 average, .406 for the Red Sox in 1941, belongs to Williams.

Phelps, the least-known member of this team, finished the 1936 season, with the Dodgers, at .367; his 319 at-bats were sufficient, under the rules of the day, for him to be runner-up to Paul Waner's league-leading .373.

OLD ACHES AND PAINS 1935
CHICAGO WHITE SOX – SHORTSTOP

Despite his nickname, Luke Appling lasted 20 seasons in the major leagues.

Face won 18 games and lost only one—all in relief—for the 1959 Pirates; his .947 won-lost percentage is the highest in history. He also had 10 saves.

The best starter would be either Ron Guidry, whose 25–3 mark for the 1978 Yankees gave him a record (for 20-game winners) .893 percentage, or Atlanta's Greg Maddux, whose .905 percentage (19–2) in 1995 is the best for pitchers with 20 decisions.

Antiquarian selections: Ross Barnes (.429 for the 1876 Cubs) at second; Hughie Jennings (.401 for the 1896 NL Baltimore Orioles) at short; and Hugh Duffy (.438 for the 1894 Braves), Tip O'Neill (.435 for the 1887 AA St. Louis Browns), and Willie Keeler (.424 for the 1897 NL Orioles) in the outfield.

The best full-season record for a twentieth-century manager is Frank Chance's .763 (116–36) with the 1906 Cubs; Cap Anson's 1880 Cubs have the best record in major league history—67 wins and 17 losses, for a .798 percentage.

Honorable mention to Walter Johnson, whose .440 average for the Senators in 1925 was the best ever by a pitcher; to Nap Lajoie, whose .422 average for the 1901 Athletics is the highest in AL history but who loses out here to Hornsby at second base; and to Ed Kranepool, whose .486 pinch-hitting average (17-for-35) for the 1974 Mets is the highest among players with at least 30 substitute at-bats in a season.

THE VERY BEST HITTERS

For all the accomplishments of the players on the two preceding teams, the most consistent hitter in the history of the game wasn't Ty Cobb or Rogers Hornsby or any of those nineteenth-century monsters who clicked off .400 averages as easily as the moderns bat .280. The greatest hitters in the history of the game—each of whom retired with perfect 1.000 batting averages—were:

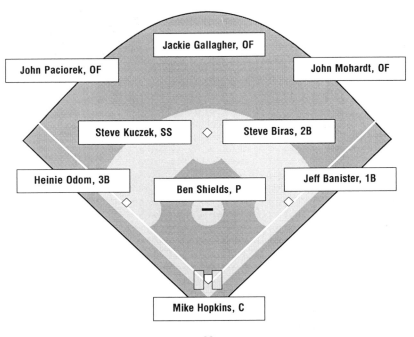

A minor league first baseman, Banister stroked a pinch-hit single in his only major league at bat, for the 1991 Pirates.

Biras is one of only five players to have 2 hits in his only 2 at bats; his 2 singles produced 2 RBIs for the Indians in 1944.

Odom singled in his only plate appearance, for the Yankees in 1925.

Kuczek interrupted his minor league career only long enough to crack a pinch-hit double for the Braves, in 1949.

Statistically the best hitter of all time is Paciorek, who went 3-for-3 with 2 walks in his only game; playing for the Astros in 1963, he also drove in 3 runs and scored 4. Back problems kept him from a second major league appearance.

Among the outfielders to go 1-for-1, Gallagher is the only one to drive in a run, for the 1923 Indians.

Mohardt (1922 Tigers) is the only 1-for-1 outfielder to score 2 runs. (He also had a walk.)

A much coveted high school prospect, John Paciorek signed with Houston for $100,000 in 1962.

Hopkins is the only position player, aside from Biras, to go 2-for-2, a single and a double for the Pirates in 1902.

It took Shields 13 appearances over four seasons (1924 and 1925 Yankees, 1930 Red Sox, and 1931 Phillies) to win more games—4—than any other pitcher without a loss; his career ERA, on the other hand, was a less-than-perfect 8.27.

The only others with 2 hits in their only 2 at-bats were pitchers Hal Deviney (1920 Red Sox), Fred Schemanske (1923 Senators), and Chet Kehn (1942 Dodgers).

Honorable mention to catcher Charlie Lindstrom of the 1958 White Sox for tripling in his only at-bat for the highest slugging percentage of all time—3.000.

Very honorable mention to baseball's only triple-threat player of perfection, John Kull, who earned a win in his only mound appearance (for the 1909 Athletics), singled in his only at bat, flawlessly handled his only chance in the field, and thus ended his career with 1.000 won-lost, batting, and fielding percentages.

MOST CAREER HOME RUNS

The top power hitters at each position—taking into account only those homers hit while playing that position—are:

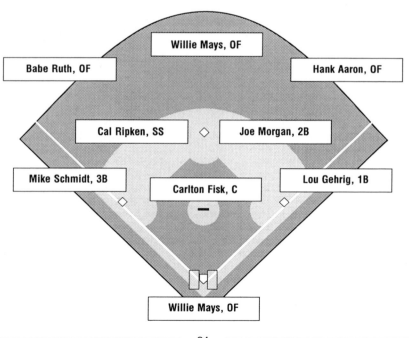

All of Gehrig's 493 home runs came while playing first base for the Yankees between 1923 and 1939.

Morgan hit 266 round-trippers as a second baseman in his twenty-two-year career (1963–84) with five clubs and 268 overall.

The difference between Schmidt's 509 home runs while playing third base (from 1972 to 1989) and the 548 he hit overall is accounted for primarily by those he hit during the 157 games he played at first.

Ripken began his major league career in 1981 as a third baseman; the games he played at the hot corner account for the difference between his 319 four-baggers at short and his lifetime total, to date, of 327.

Ruth's slugging began while he was still a pitcher; his mound appearances and the handful of games in which he played first base explain the difference between his 692 homers as an outfielder and his overall figure of 714 (from 1914 to 1935 for the Red Sox, Yankees, and Braves).

Home-run king Hank Aaron pictured tying Babe Ruth's mark of 714 round-trippers.

Aaron played 210 games at first base and ended his career (1954–76 for the Braves in Milwaukee and Atlanta, and the Brewers) with 202 appearances as a designated hitter (DH); he recorded only 661 of his record 755 home runs as an outfielder.

Mays reached the fences enough times while filling in at first base to raise his total of homers as an outfielder—643—to 660 in his twenty-two seasons (1951–73) with the Giants on both coasts and the Mets.

Fisk connected enough times as a DH and while exiled to various infield and outfield positions for the Red Sox and White Sox in his twenty-three seasons (between 1969 and 1992) to run his numbers up from 351 as a backstop to 375.

Ferrell connected once as a pinch hitter to add to his total of 37 as a pitcher for six teams from 1927 to 1941.

The most obvious exclusion resulting from the rigid requirements of this lineup is Ernie Banks, who hit only 277 of his 512 homers as a shortstop.

MOST HOME RUNS IN A SEASON

Several very deserving heavy hitters get excluded from this lineup on technicalities.

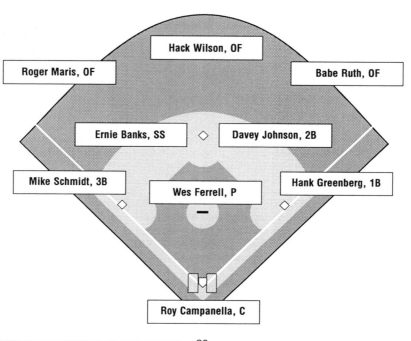

Hack Wilson, OF

Roger Maris, OF

Babe Ruth, OF

Ernie Banks, SS

Davey Johnson, 2B

Mike Schmidt, 3B

Wes Ferrell, P

Hank Greenberg, 1B

Roy Campanella, C

Greenberg connected for 58 round-trippers for the 1938 Tigers.

Johnson homered 42 times while playing second base for the 1973 Braves.

Schmidt clouted 48 four-baggers for the 1980 Phillies.

Banks hit 47 for the 1958 Cubs.

Maris, of course, holds the major league record for any position—61 for the 1961 Yankees.

Right behind Maris is Ruth, who knocked 60 for the Yankees in 1927.

The NL record belongs to Wilson, who blasted 56 for the Cubs in 1930.

Campanella's 40 circuit blasts for the 1953 Dodgers marked the only time any player reached that mark while in the lineup as a receiver.

Ferrell helped himself with 9 round-trippers while pitching for the 1931 Indians.

Four footnotes:

Jimmie Foxx (1932 Athletics) tied Greenberg, but he hit some of his 58 homers while playing 13 games at third base.

A three-time National League MVP, Roy Campanella reached the 20-homer mark seven timers in his ten-year career.

Rogers Hornsby (1922 Cardinals) matched Johnson's 42 round-trippers, but since Johnson added one as a pinch hitter, he makes the cut.

Ruth deserves to be on this team twice, the second time for his 59 homers in 1921.

Johnny Bench's home run total for the 1970 Reds was 45, which looks good enough to make this team behind the plate, but six of his blasts came while he was playing the outfield, and he hit one while penciled in as a first baseman. Also, Campanella added a forty-first pinch-hitting.

If we had been looking for a pitcher to stop all these power hitters, we could have done worse than Allen Sothoron, who, while working for the Browns, Red Sox, and Indians in 1921, established a record for hurling 178 1/3 innings without giving up a single homer.

LONGEST BATTING STREAKS

Consistency is the hallmark of a great hitter—or at least of a good hitter in the middle of a hot streak. This lineup includes the players who hit safely at least once in the most consecutive games.

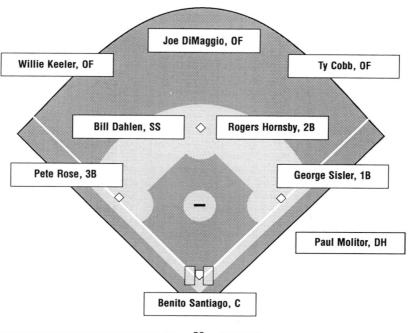

DiMaggio, of course, holds the major league record of 56 consecutive games, a feat he accomplished for the 1941 Yankees. After him come Keeler (1897 NL Baltimore Orioles) and Rose (1978 Reds), 44; Dahlen (1894 Cubs), 42; Sisler (1922 Browns), 41; Cobb (1911 Tigers), 40; Molitor (1987 Brewers), 39; and Santiago (1987 Padres), 34.

The least predictable names in this lineup are those of the shortstop and the catcher. In fact, there have been only sixteen hitting streaks of 34 or more games in the history of baseball, and Dahlen and Santiago are the only players at their positions to reach that mark.

Dahlen compiled a .272 average for four NL teams in a twenty-one-year career (1891–1911). He batted over .300 only twice, and 1894, the year NL batting averages exploded as a result of the increase in the distance between pitcher and batter from fifty feet to sixty feet six inches, was a career year for him: a .362 average, 15 home runs, and 107 RBIs (the only occasion on which he reached double digits in homers or the century mark in RBIs).

COBB, DETROIT

Only Ty Cobb has chalked up three, or even two, batting streaks of 34 or more games.

Santiago joined this team by setting a rookie-record batting streak. He hit an even .300 in 1987 and set personal-high marks in doubles and homers. Since then, he has hit as high as .280 only once.

Honorable mention to Tommy Holmes (37 straight games with a hit for the 1945 Braves), Billy Hamilton (36, for the 1894 Phillies), Fred Clarke (35, for the NL's Louisville club in 1897), George McQuinn (34, for the 1938 Browns), and Dom DiMaggio (34, for the 1949 Red Sox).

Cobb is the only player to put together more than one hitting streak of at least 34 consecutive games; in 1917 he assembled a streak of 35 games; in 1912, another of 34 contests.

OTHER GAME STREAKS

The members of this squad may not have gotten a hit every day, but each of them had the longest streak of one sort or another.

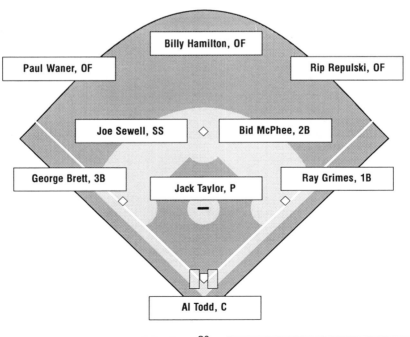

Grimes drove in at least one run in 17 consecutive games for the 1922 Cubs.

McPhee played his first 1,695 games, for the Reds in both the AA and the NL, before becoming, on Opening Day in 1896, the last player to yield to the fad of using a glove in the field.

Brett had 6 consecutive 3-hit games for the Royals in 1976.

In 1929, while with the Indians, Sewell went 115 straight games without striking out.

Hamilton scored a run for the Phillies in 24 straight contests in 1894.

Waner stroked at least one extra base hit in 14 straight games for the 1927 Pirates.

Repulski stroked at least 2 hits in 10 straight appearances for the Cardinals in 1954.

Todd set up behind the plate without allowing a passed ball in a record 128 games for the 1937 Pirates.

JOE SEWELL
CLEVELAND INDIANS – SHORTSTOP   1922

Joe Sewell struck out less frequently than any other players in major league history.

Taylor holds what is arguably the least approachable baseball record—188 straight complete games, for the Cubs and Cardinals, between 1901 and 1906.

Honorable mention to:

Roy Cullenbine (1947 Tigers) for working pitchers for a base on balls in 22 consecutive contests.

Dave Philley (1958–59 Phillies) for his 9 consecutive successful pinch-hitting appearances.

Dale Long (1956 Pirates), Don Mattingly (1987 Yankees), and Ken Griffey Jr. (1993 Mariners) for homering in 8 consecutive games.

And Carl Hubbell (1936–37 Giants) for chalking up a victory in 24 straight decisions.

Although they are streaks of a different sort, worthy of mention are the 12 consecutive hits of Walt Dropo (1952 Tigers) and Pinky Higgins (1938 Red Sox) and the 16 consecutive times on base of Ted Williams (1957 Red Sox).

BACK-TO-BACK MOST VALUABLE PLAYERS (MVPS)

Only eleven players have won the MVP Award in consecutive seasons. The first nine were:

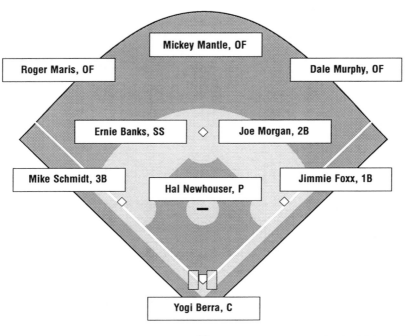

Foxx won his awards while with the Athletics in 1932 and 1933.

Morgan earned his in 1975 and 1976 for the Big Red Machine of Cincinnati.

Schmidt's pair of trophies came in 1980 and 1981 with the Phillies; the third baseman added another award in 1986.

Banks didn't let back-to-back fifth-place finishes by the Cubs deter him from winning the award in 1958 and 1959.

Mantle's first two MVPs helped the Yankees win pennants in 1956 and 1957.

So did Maris's in 1960 and 1961.

Murphy's two banner years (1982 and 1983, while he was with the Braves) are perhaps the least remembered of those on this squad.

The Yankees' Berra took the award in 1954 and 1955; he had won an earlier prize in 1951.

Newhouser (1944 and 1945 Tigers) was the best pitcher of the World War II years.

Foxx (1938 Red Sox), Schmidt (1986 Phillies), Mantle (1962 Yankees), and Berra (1951 Yankees) each turned the hat trick and won a third MVP Award.

HAL NEWHOUSER
DETROIT TIGERS – PITCHER   1940

Hal Newhouser won 80 games between 1944 and 1946, but was kept out of the Hall of Fame until 1992 because his best seasons came during talent-impoverished World War II years.

The most recent back-to-back winners are Frank Thomas (1993 and 1994 White Sox) and Barry Bonds. Bonds took the award in 1990 and 1992, while with the Pirates, then, after signing with the Giants as a free agent, earned a third trophy in 1993.

The only others to win as many as three MVPs, although never two in a row, are Joe DiMaggio (1939, 1941, and 1947 Yankees); Stan Musial (1943, 1946, and 1948 Cardinals); and Roy Campanella (1951, 1953, and 1955 Dodgers).

Honorable mention to Greg Maddux, the only pitcher to win four (or even three) consecutive Cy Young Awards. The righthander copped his first prize, for the Cubs, in 1992 and followed that up with three more for the Braves. Before Maddux, only Steve Carlton (1972, 1977, 1980, and 1982 Phillies) had been awarded the Cy Young trophy as many as four times.

STREAK BREAKERS

It wasn't so much what these players did as when they did it.

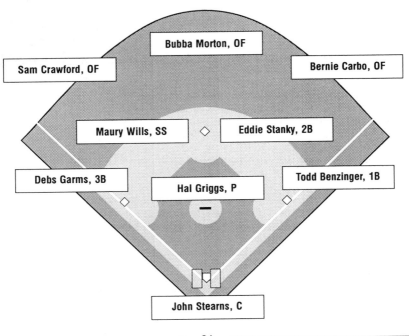

Bubba Morton, OF

Sam Crawford, OF

Bernie Carbo, OF

Maury Wills, SS

Eddie Stanky, 2B

Debs Garms, 3B

Todd Benzinger, 1B

Hal Griggs, P

John Stearns, C

The Dodgers' Orel Hershiser ran his record string of 59 consecutive scoreless innings through the tenth inning of his final start of 1988. On Opening Day the next April, however, he gave up a run-scoring single to Cincinnati's Benzinger in the first inning.

In 1947, Ewell Blackwell came within two outs of duplicating Johnny Vander Meer's consecutive no-hitters. Four days after holding the Braves hitless on June 18, the Cincinnati righthander set down the Dodgers until Stanky's one-out single in the ninth.

In the start following his no-hitters in 1938, Cincinnati southpaw Vander Meer held the Braves hitless until Garms connected safely with two out in the fourth.

Tom Seaver of the Mets struck out the last 10 San Diego batters of his 19-whiff masterpiece on April 22, 1970. Leading off for the Dodgers in the righthander's next start, Wills broke the streak simply by putting the ball in play.

Sam Crawford holds the all-time major league mark for his 312 triples.

Cy Young holds the mark for most consecutive hitless innings—23, over 4 games, including a perfect game. The streak ended in the seventh inning on May 11, 1904, when Detroit's Crawford touched the Boston righthander for a hit.

When the otherwise unillustrious Morton worked Bill Fischer for a base on balls on September 30, 1962, the Detroit outfielder ended the righthander's 84 1/3 consecutive innings without giving up a walk.

San Francisco's Jim Barr retired the last 21 batters he faced on August 23, 1972, and the first 20 he faced in his next game. The twenty-first was the Cardinals' Carbo, who doubled to end the longest string of consecutive batsmen retired by a major league pitcher.

One of Stearns's 4 home runs in 1982 halted Greg Minton's record 269 1/3 consecutive innings without giving up a four-bagger. The San Francisco righthander recorded 70 saves over the three seasons (1980–82) covered by the streak.

A righthander with a 6–26 record in a four-year career with the Senators, Griggs got Ted Williams to ground out to second in his first at-bat on September 24, 1957, after the Red Sox' slugger had reached base in 16 consecutive plate appearances (2 singles, 4 homers, 9 walks, and a hit by the pitch). Williams later homered to win the game.

MAJOR FEATS IN THE MINORS

Some things that have never happened in the major leagues did take place in the minors.

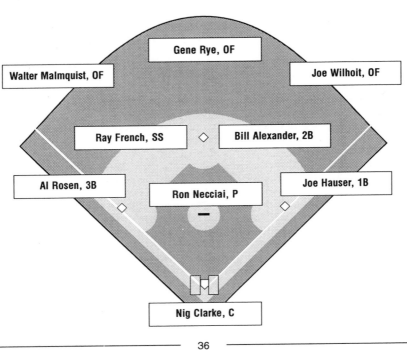

Gene Rye, OF

Walter Malmquist, OF

Joe Wilhoit, OF

Ray French, SS

Bill Alexander, 2B

Al Rosen, 3B

Joe Hauser, 1B

Ron Necciai, P

Nig Clarke, C

Hauser is the only player to hit more than 60 home runs in a season twice—63 with the International League (IL) Baltimore Orioles in 1930 and 69 for Minneapolis of the AA in 1933. After seasons in which he hit as high as .323 (1922) and slugged as many as 27 homers (1924), the lefty swinger was slated for stardom with Connie Mack's Philadelphia Athletics. But a freak broken leg in spring training in 1925 sent him back to the minors for most of the rest of his career, and a fractured kneecap in 1934 curtailed his effectiveness even at that level.

Ron Necciai pitched baseball's dream game.

Alexander went 8-for-8 in a game for Corsicana of the Texas League on June 15, 1902; he never played in the majors.

In 1948, Rosen hit 5 consecutive homers over 2 games for Kansas City of the AA. The righthanded slugger had a ten-year major league career with the Indians, during which he led the AL in slugging, homers, runs batted in, and runs scored in various seasons.

Luis Aparicio holds the major league record for appearing in 2,581 games at shortstop, but French played short 2,736 times over a twenty-eight-year minor league career, from 1914 to 1941, mostly in the Pacific Coast League (PCL). Like Aparicio, he was reputedly a superlative fielder, and he batted 5 points higher (.267 to .262) than the Hall of Famer. Unlike Aparicio, his big league career was limited to 82 games with three teams over three seasons (the 1920 Yankees, 1923 Dodgers, and 1924 White Sox). Never a great hitter, his big league average was only .193, but he hung around the minors long enough to collect 3,254 hits.

Malmquist hit .477 for York of the Nebraska State League in 1913, the highest average in a professional league since the founding of the NL in 1876; he never reached the major leagues.

On August 6, 1930, Rye, while playing for Waco of the Texas League, hit 3 homers in the eighth inning of a game against Beaumont. Waco scored 18 runs in Rye's big inning and won the contest 22–4. Born Eugene Mercantelli, the lefty hitter's major league career consisted of 17 games for the Red Sox in 1931; in that time he managed only 7 singles for a .179 average.

Wilhoit's 69-game batting streak for Wichita of the Western League in 1920 is a professional record. His major league career—with the Braves, Pirates, Giants, and Red Sox—had ended before the streak; he hit .257 in 283 big league games between 1916 and 1919.

Clarke was Alexander's teammate in 1902. On the same day that the second baseman got his 8 hits, the catcher banged out 8 home runs in 8 at-bats and drove in 16 runs as Corsicana obliterated Texarkana by the preposterous score of 51–3. The left-handed hitter spent all or part of nine years in the bigs (1905–11 with the Tigers, Indians, and Browns and 1919–20 with the Phillies and Pirates); in 506 games he managed only 6 homers.

On May 13, 1952, just a month shy of his twentieth birthday, Necciai pitched the dream game, striking out 27 batters in a 7–0 no-hitter for Bristol of the Appalachian League. Since one batter had grounded out in the second inning, it took a passed ball by the catcher on the twenty-sixth strikeout to give the righthander the opportunity to record number 27. After striking out 281 minor league batters in 169 innings (with Burlington of the Carolina League as well as with Bristol), he was promoted to the parent Pirates to add a gate attraction to the end of a lackluster last-place season. With Pittsburgh, he struck out 31 batters in 54 2/3 innings, compiled a 1–6 record, and racked up an earned-run average (ERA) of 7.08.

Honorable mentions to other minor leaguers who hold a variety of professional records:

Joe Cantwell, who hit 3 grand slams in a 1914 game for Opelika of the Georgia-Alabama League. He never played in the majors.

Jack Dunn, owner-manager of the IL Baltimore Orioles, won seven consecutive pennants between 1919 and 1925.

Ike Boone, whose .370 career minor league batting average over fourteen seasons (between 1920 and 1937) is 3 points higher than Ty Cobb's major league mark and whose 553 total bases for the 1929 San Francisco Missions of the PCL are the most by any player in a professional league. The lefty swinger played all or part of eight seasons in the majors, hitting .319; in the two seasons in which he appeared in more than 100 big league games (1924 and 1925, for the Red Sox), he batted .333 and .330.

Spencer Harris, who scored 2,287 minor league runs (42 more than Cobb scored in the majors). A slap-hitting lefty, he never made it to the majors but played twenty-eight seasons (1921–48) in the minors, setting all-time bush-league marks in hits, doubles, total bases, and walks as well as runs scored.

Buzz Arlett, who clouted 4 homers in a game twice for the IL Baltimore Orioles in 1932. The switch hitter was one of the rare one-season regulars in the majors, batting .313 for the 1931 Phillies.

Bill Kennedy, who struck out 456 batters in 280 innings for Rocky Mount of the Coastal Plains League in 1946; the southpaw won 28 and lost 3, with a 1.03 ERA. In eight big league seasons in the late 1940s and 1950s, Kennedy had 256 strikeouts in 464 2/3 innings while winning 15 and losing 28 and giving up 4.71 earned runs every 9 innings.

Bill Bell, Necciai's teammate in 1952, who hurled three no-hitters during the season. Like Necciai, he was rushed to the majors and lost one game without winning any in parts of two seasons with the Pirates.

Joe Bauman, who hit 72 home runs for Rosewell of the Longhorn League in 1954. He never made it to the big leagues.

Bob Crues, who drove in 254 runs for Amarillo in the West Texas–New Mexico League in 1954. Despite his prodigious slugging, he never earned a promotion to the majors.

Bob Riesener, who compiled a spotless 20–0 record for Alexandria in the Evangeline League in 1957; his career ended at the minor league level.

WORST CAREER HITTERS

Anyone who doubts that expansion has a generally adverse effect on the major league talent pool should consider the following:

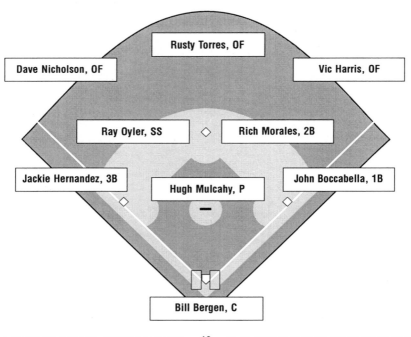

Bergen is statistically the worst hitter with any significant longevity in the history of baseball. Between 1901 and 1911 he came to bat 3,028 times for the Reds and Dodgers and compiled a shockingly paltry .170 batting average.

The records of his teammates, each of whom had at least 1,000 at-bats, are:

Boccabella, .219 for three NL teams from 1963 to 1974;

Morales, .195 for the White Sox and Padres between 1967 and 1974;

Hernandez, .208 for four clubs from 1965 to 1973;

Oyler, .175 for three AL squads between 1965 and 1970, including an unimpressive .135 in 215 at-bats for the Tigers in 1968;

Nicholson, .212 for four teams in seven seasons between 1960 and 1967;

Jackie Hernandez began his career with 2 hits in his first six at-bats; from there it was all downhill.

Torres, .212 in nine seasons on five AL rosters between 1971 and 1980;

Harris, .217 in eight seasons (between 1972 and 1980) with five franchises.

Mulcahy won the sobriquet "Losing Pitcher" for his 45–89 record (a .336 percentage) with the Phillies and Pirates over nine seasons, interrupted by World War II.

Deserving dishonorable mention for his 42 wins and 83 losses (a slightly worse percentage than Mulcahy's) is Rollie Naylor, who labored unproductively for the Athletics between 1917 and 1924. Worse still is Jim Hughey, but he suffered through his 29–80 (.266) career—for five teams in seven seasons—at the end of the last century.

The worst managerial record among pilots with 1,000 games in the majors belongs to Jimmie Wilson; he compiled a .401 percentage (493 victories and 735 losses) for the Phillies and Cubs in the 1930s and 1940s.

The only other major leaguers with at least 1,000 at-bats and batting averages below .200 are catchers Fritz Buelow (.192 from 1899 to 1907) and Mike Ryan (.193 from 1964 to 1974).

As for the effect of adding teams to the big leagues: Every one of the position players mentioned here was active during an expansion period (the creation of the AL in the cases of Bergen and Buelow).

WORST SINGLE-SEASON HITTERS

Although he turned in such unglamorous yearly batting averages as .132, .139, and .159, Bill Bergen's managers never allowed him quite enough plate appearances to qualify for a batting title. The worst hitters who did have a minimum of 400 at-bats in a season are:

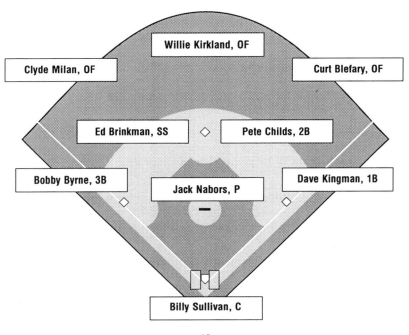

Kingman (1982 Mets) managed to lead the NL in home runs while batting a mere .204.

Childs finished the 1902 season with a .194 average for the Phillies.

Byrne clocked in at .191 for the 1908 Cardinals.

Brinkman's consistency for the 1965 Senators was the worst ever: His batting average had to be rounded off to reach .185.

Milan (1909 Senators), Kirkland (1962 Indians), and Blefary (1968 Orioles) all finished right on the Mendoza Line at exactly .200.

Sullivan ended the 1908 season for the White Sox with a .191 percentage.

Despite a 3.47 ERA, Nabors posted a 1–20 record with the 1916 Athletics—the lowest single-season won-lost percentage (.048) in history.

Among the position players, Brinkman has the most competition: His average was .1847 against John Gochnaur's back-to-back .1852 in 1902 and .1849 in 1903; considering Gochnaur's twentieth-century record of 98 errors in the latter season, it is arguable that he had the worst season ever by a major leaguer. Also deserving mention is Dal Maxvill, who,

Ed Brinkman's glove kept him in the big leagues for fifteen years; in fact, he once held the record for most consecutive errorless games by a shortstop.

although he failed to come up with the qualifying 400 at-bats for the 1969 Cardinals, used his 372 official plate appearances to compile an eyeball-popping .175 average.

Nabors's neighbors are his roommate on the 1916 A's, Tom Sheehan, who was only slightly better, with a 1–16 record (.059); John Coleman, who won 12 but who set the single-season loss record of 48 for the 1883 Phillies, and Gene Garber, whose 16 losses for the 1979 Braves are the most ever suffered by a relief pitcher.

Connie Mack's 1916 Athletics had the worst won-lost percentage of all the clubs that went through a season with only one pilot; the last-place A's finished with 36 wins and 117 losses—a .235 percentage.

Honorable mention to Mike Jordan, the only player ever to bat 100 times without reaching a .100 average. In his only major league season (1890), the Pittsburgh outfielder managed 11 singles and one double in 125 at-bats for an .096 average.

THE VERY WORST

Randy Tate, a pitcher for the 1975 Mets, went hitless in 41 at-bats to establish the standard for offensive futility. But, as the following team illustrates, not all career .000 averages belong to pitchers.

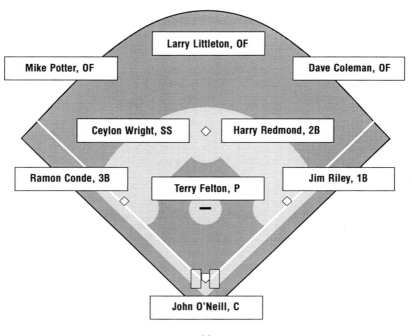

Riley went hitless in 11 at-bats for the Browns in 1921, then, with the Senators two years later, he added 3 more at-bats to his hitless career total.

Harry Redmond had the second-highest number of at-bats without a safety—19, for the 1909 Dodgers.

Conde was 0-for-16 with the 1962 White Sox.

Wright's futility lasted through 18 plate appearances, including 7 strikeouts, for the 1916 White Sox. Defensively he was a bust as well, committing 5 errors in 32 chances, for an .844 fielding percentage.

Potter (1976–77 Cardinals) set the standard for position players, with 23 hitless at-bats in his understandably brief career.

Littleton matched Potter's total, for the Indians in 1981.

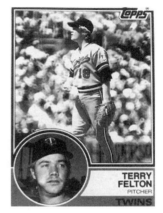

TERRY FELTON
PITCHER
TWINS

While Terry Felton never won a major league game, he did record three saves.

There are other outfielders who went 0-for-12 in their careers, but Coleman struck out three times in the process.

O'Neill had two cups of coffee with the Giants (in 1899 and 1902), neither of them very hot; he holds a big league record for failing to reach base on a hit or walk in 15 tries.

Felton's 0–16 won-lost record is the worst by a pitcher without a victory; he did his unproductive hurling for the Twins between 1979 and 1982, compiling an ERA of 5.53.

Comanagers for this squad are George Creamer (1884 AA Pittsburgh Alleghenys) and Moose Stubing (1988 Angels), both of whom managed for 8 games and lost them all.

Honorable mention to Paul Dicken for his 0–13 strictly as a pinch hitter for the 1964 and 1966 Indians.

To righthander Bob Buhl, whose 0-for-70 is the worst single-season (1962 Braves and Cubs) batting record. (His career average was a relatively lofty .089.)

And to catcher Hal Finney, whose 0–35 for the 1936 Pirates is unapproached for one-year lack of productivity among position players, even though he managed to bat .203 overall in his five-year career.

POWER SHORTAGE

A lineup of players who never hit a home run despite a substantial number of at-bats:

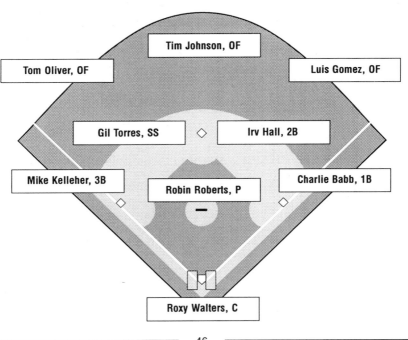

Babb batted 1,180 times for the Giants and Dodgers between 1903 and 1905.

Hall came to the plate 1,904 times for the Athletics from 1943 to 1946.

Kelleher hit 1,081 times for five teams from 1972 to 1982.

Torres came to bat 1,271 times for the Senators in a four-year career pre– and post–World War II.

The ultimate slap hitter, Oliver (1930–33 Red Sox) had more homerless at-bats—1,931—than any other major leaguer; he did, however, hit .277 in his career.

Johnson's power drought lasted through 1,269 plate appearances for the Brewers and Blue Jays from 1973 to 1979.

Gomez never got to trot around the bases in 1,251 plate appearances for three teams from 1974 to 1981.

Walters came up to the plate on 1,426 occasions for the Yankees, Red Sox, and Indians from 1915 to 1925.

Robin Roberts's penchant for giving up the long ball didn't prevent him from winning 286 games.

Hall of Famer Roberts gave up more four-baggers—505—than any other pitcher.

Johnson and Gomez were primarily infielders, but each of them appeared in the outfield twice. Purists who prefer outfield specialists will have to settle for Rip Cannell (913 at-bats for the Red Sox in 1904 and 1905) and Marty Callaghan (767 at-bats for the Cubs and Reds in a four-year career dragged out between 1922 and 1930).

The only other player with 1,000 or more homerless at-bats is infielder Red Shannon (1,070, with five teams in seven seasons between 1915 and 1926).

Honorable mention to Tommy Thevenow, a shortstop for five NL clubs from 1924 to 1938. The .247 hitter's only 2 homers (both in 1926) were of the inside-the-park variety, giving him the undisputed record of 4,164 at-bats without ever clearing a major league fence. He failed to circle the bases at all in the final 3,347 at-bats of his career, a record that appears all but unapproachable.

Hall of Famer Rabbit Maranville holds the record for most homerless at-bats in a season—672, for the 1922 Pirates.

HELPLESS HANDS

When it comes to RBIs for a season, these players have been the most unproductive during a minimum of 400 at-bats:

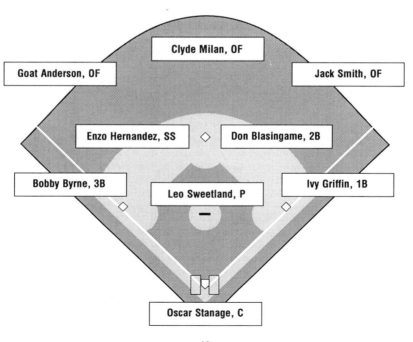

Clyde Milan, OF

Goat Anderson, OF

Jack Smith, OF

Enzo Hernandez, SS

Don Blasingame, 2B

Bobby Byrne, 3B

Leo Sweetland, P

Ivy Griffin, 1B

Oscar Stanage, C

Hernandez's 12 RBIs in 549 at-bats in his rookie season for San Diego in 1971 is by far the least productive season in history. Although he never descended to such depths again, he also never qualified as anyone's idea of a threat with men in scoring position, driving home only 113 runs in 2,327 at-bats over eight big league seasons. On the other hand, he had lots of company in his pace-setting season: Second baseman Don Mason had only 11 RBIs in 344 at-bats for the 1971 Padres, and catcher Bob Barton managed to knock home only 25 runs in 376 official plate appearances.

The RBI totals for Hernandez's teammates in this lineup are:

Over his eight-year career, Enzo Hernandez drove in only 113 runs in 2,327 at-bats.

   Griffin, 20 for the 1920 Athletics;
   Blasingame, 18 for the 1965 Senators;
   Byrne, 14 for the 1908 Cardinals;
   Anderson, 12 for the 1907 Pirates;
   Milan, 15 for the 1909 Senators;
   Smith, 15 for the 1919 Cardinals;
   Stanage, 25 for the 1914 Tigers.

Byrne deserves additional comment, since he was among the more punchless of the Punchless Wonders, the 1907 Cardinals, who scored a meager 371 runs, the lowest total since major league teams adopted a schedule that exceeded 100 games in the 1880s.

Almost as helpless were Milan's 1909 Senators, whose 380 runs were the fewest scored in AL history. The RBI team leader was Bob Unglaub with 41, and he was a utility player who filled in all over the diamond for less productive teammates.

Sweetland's 7.71 ERA for the Phillies in 1930, the Year of the Hitter, is the highest for any hurler who qualified for the category title. Claude Willoughby, his teammate on what was the worst pitching staff in the annals of baseball, just missed being the runner-up, with a 7.59 mark, only because he fell one inning short of the required 154 frames. The staff that Sweetland anchored gave up record numbers of runs (1,199) and hits (1,993) and an all-time-high opponents' batting average of .346.

MOST CAREER STRIKEOUTS

Strikeouts kill rallies but not necessarily careers. Each of these players is of relatively recent vintage, and each had sufficient power to make the whiffs almost incidental.

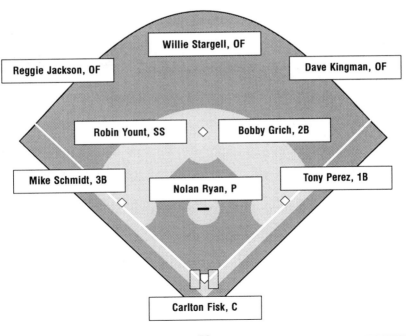

The top three strikeout totals in baseball history belong to Hall of Famers: Jackson's 2,597 (for the A's in both Kansas City and Oakland, Orioles, Yankees, and Angels from 1967 to 1987), Stargell's 1,936 (for the Pirates from 1962 to 1982), and Schmidt's 1,883 (for the Phillies from 1972 to 1989).

The totals for the rest of the lineup are:

Perez, 1,867 (1964–86, Reds, Expos, Red Sox, and Phillies);

Grich, 1,278 (1970–86, Orioles and Angels);

Yount, 1,350 (1974–93, Brewers);

Kingman, 1,816 (1971–86, Giants, Mets, Padres, Angels, Yankees, Cubs, and A's);

Fisk, 1,386 (1969, 1971–93, Red Sox and White Sox).

Ryan merits inclusion here because he holds the record for most walks—2,795, over a twenty-seven-year career (between 1966 and 1993) with the Mets, Angels, Astros, and Rangers. Of course, he also holds the career mark for most strikeouts—5,714.

Willie Stargell holds the National League record for most strikeouts.

Dishonorable mention to outfielder Bobby Bonds, whose sixth-ranking 1,757 K's are not enough to make this team but whose 189 with the 1970 Giants and 187 a year earlier are the two highest one-season marks in history.

The highest strikeout average on this team, .272, belongs to Kingman. He and Jackson finished their careers with more K's than hits, but neither can hold a candle to Rob Deer's astonishing .360 (1,379 whiffs in 3,831 at-bats). Deer's lifetime batting average from 1984 to 1993, on the other hand, was only .220.

Another nod, to champion free swinger Tony Armas (1976–89), who owns the highest ratio of strikeouts (1,201) to walks (260)—better than four and a half to one—among players with 4,000 or more at-bats.

Armas's mound counterpart, Tom Zachary (1918–36), has the worst ratio of walks (914) to strikeouts (720) among pitchers who have hurled at least 3,000 innings.

TRANSACTION FIRSTS

These players were all involved in the first instance of one kind of transaction or another.

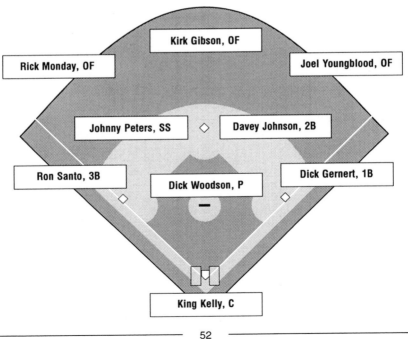

Kirk Gibson, OF

Rick Monday, OF

Joel Youngblood, OF

Johnny Peters, SS

Davey Johnson, 2B

Ron Santo, 3B

Dick Woodson, P

Dick Gernert, 1B

King Kelly, C

The Red Sox swap of Gernert to the Cubs for Jim Marshall and Dave Hillman in 1959 marked the first modern interleague trade not requiring waivers.

When he signed with the Phillies in 1977, Johnson became the first player to return to the majors from Japan.

In 1970, Santo was the first to exercise his so-called Woolworth rights (five years with the same club, ten years in the majors) when he refused a trade from the Cubs to the Angels; he eventually accepted a deal that sent him to the White Sox.

Peters was the original "player to be named later," going to Providence from the Cubs for catcher Lew Brown in 1880.

The Athletics made Monday the first pick in the first amateur draft, in 1965.

Youngblood was the first player to get hits for two teams in two cities on the same day; traded by New York to Montreal for pitcher Tom Gorman after a day game at Wrigley Field on August 4, 1982, the outfielder hopped a plane in time to join the Expos for a game that night.

Rick Monday played for 19 seasons, with the A's, Cubs, and Dodgers, but a bad back prevented him from achieving the stardom predicted for him.

Gibson was the first second-look free agent to switch teams (from the Tigers to the Dodgers) after the 1988 collusion settlement between the players and owners.

Kelly's sale to the Braves in 1887 netted the Cubs $10,000 in the first cash transaction for a major league player.

In 1974, Woodson became the first player to go to salary arbitration; he won his case against the Twins.

The manager for this squad comes from a unique swap of pilots and coaches that saw Cleveland dugout boss Joe Gordon and assistant Joe Moore go to the Tigers in exchange for their Detroit counterparts, Jimmy Dykes and Luke Appling, in 1960.

Honorable mentions: Outfielders Max Flack of the Cubs and Cliff Heathcote of the Cardinals were traded for each other between games of a doubleheader on May 30, 1922; each played for both teams that day. Reliever Bill Campbell departed the Twins for the Red Sox after the 1976 season to become the first regular free-agent signee.

WORST TRADES

A team will often give up a valuable player because it needs money. But the members of this lineup were allowed to get away in exchange for lesser players without the added benefit of some quick cash.

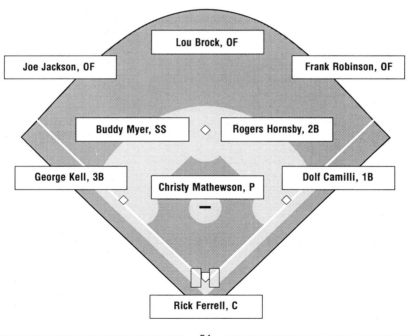

Lou Brock, OF

Joe Jackson, OF

Frank Robinson, OF

Buddy Myer, SS

Rogers Hornsby, 2B

George Kell, 3B

Christy Mathewson, P

Dolf Camilli, 1B

Rick Ferrell, C

Failing to see the sophomore Camilli's potential, the Cubs traded him to the Phillies in June 1934 for a washed-up Don Hurst, who lasted only 51 games with Chicago before retiring. The lefty hitter went on to a twelve-year career in which he hit .277, with enough power to bang out at least 23 homers in eight consecutive seasons and drive in more than 100 runs five times.

To prove that he suffered no rivals to his authority, manager John McGraw rid himself of Hornsby after only one season (1927), in which the future Hall of Famer hit .361; as compensation, the Braves had to send the Giants only catcher Shanty Hogan and outfielder Jimmy Welsh.

Kell was only slightly more than two years into his Hall of Fame career when the Athletics traded him to the Tigers for Barney McCosky in May 1946. The outfielder turned in four .300 seasons for Philadelphia, then faded dramatically before drifting around the major leagues until 1953; before retiring in 1957,

George Kell's American League–leading .343 average in 1949 deprived Ted Williams of an unprecedented third Triple Crown.

Kell had eight .300 seasons for Detroit, including a batting crown in 1949, and three more after leaving them.

Washington owner Clark Griffith called his 1927 shortstop-for-shortstop trade of Buddy Myer for Topper Rigney the worst of his career. Rigney lasted all of 45 games with the Senators, and Myer went on to a seventeen-year career in which he hit .303. Fortunately for Griffith, he got Myer back from the Red Sox after only a year and a half for players named Milt Gaston, Hod Lisenbee, Bobby Reeves, Grant Gillis, and Elliott Bigelow in what was one of the worst deals in Boston history.

Jackson, of Black Sox infamy, holds the highest batting average of any non–Hall of Famer (.356). Even though he recognized the lefty swinger's abilities, Connie Mack traded him to the Indians in July 1910 for outfielder Bris Lord (a .256 lifetime hitter) because the country-born Jackson was too intimidated by big-city Philadelphia to play up to his potential.

Hall of Famer Brock collected 3,023 base hits and stole 938 bases, almost all of them after the Cubs traded him (along with two inconsequential pitchers) to the Cardinals in June 1964 for pitchers Ernie Broglio and Bobby Shantz (a combined 15–33 record for Chicago) and outfielder Doug Clemens (a lifetime .229 hitter).

The Reds traded Robinson to the Orioles in December 1965 because he was, in the words of Cincinnati owner Bill DeWitt, "an old thirty." The outfielder went on to win the Triple Crown and the AL MVP in 1966, to lead Baltimore to four pennants, and to earn a plaque in Cooperstown. After moving to Cincinnati in the trade, Milt Pappas went on to the second half of a seventeen-year journeyman career (209–164), Jack Baldschun won only 9 games, and outfielder Dick Simpson remained as obscure as he had been.

In May 1933, the Browns shipped future Hall of Famer Ferrell to the Red Sox, for whom he hit around .300 over four seasons and teamed with his brother Wes for the best sibling battery in baseball history; in return, St. Louis picked up receiver Merv Shea, a career .220 hitter—and threw in hurler Lloyd Brown and some cash for the honor.

The single worst one-for-one trade in the history of the game featured two Hall of Fame righthanders. On December 15, 1900, the Giants sent Amos Rusie, who had won 234 games in the 1890s despite missing all of 1896 in a holdout and all of 1899 and 1900 due to a shoulder injury, to Cincinnati for a rookie. The first-year player was Christy Mathewson, who went on to a NL-record 373 victories; Rusie ended his career by appearing in only 3 games for the Reds, losing one game without a win. The rest of the story is that Cincinnati owner John T. Brush, who engineered the deal, was at the same time negotiating for the purchase of the Giants; the Rusie-Mathewson deal may have been the worst in Cincinnati history, but for Brush it was the best of his career.

By far the most lopsided trade of all time was a product of another form of collusion. In December 1899, Barney Dreyfuss, the owner of the NL Louisville Colonels, purchased a half share of the Pirates. Simultaneously, he announced that his old club was sending future Hall of Famers Honus Wagner and Fred Clarke, third baseman Tommy Leach (a career .270 hitter), second baseman Claude Ritchey (.273), catcher Chief Zimmer (.269), and pitchers Deacon Phillippe (189–107 lifetime) and Rube Waddell (191–145) to the Pirates for Jack Chesbro and three other nonentities. It surprised no one when Louisville was one of the four teams cut from the NL before the start of the 1900 season and Chesbro wound up back in Pittsburgh.

Other classic bum deals:

When the Red Sox sent outfielder George Stone to the Browns for Jesse Burkett in January 1905, they got a future Hall of Famer with a career batting average of .339 but one who hit a mere .257 in his final season. What they gave up was the AL leader in base hits in 1905, the batting champion of 1906, and a career .301 hitter over the next six years.

Nellie Fox for Joe Tipton looked like a toss-up for the Athletics and White Sox in October 1949. A decade and a half later, catcher Tipton had been retired for ten years (with a .236 career average); Fox, on the other hand, had given Chicago a lifetime .288 average and was the AL's best second baseman of the 1950s and early 1960s.

Just before the 1960 season started, the Indians sent first baseman Norm Cash to the Tigers for third baseman Steve Demeter. In his seventeen-year career, Cash hit .277, including a batting crown in 1961, and stroked 377 homers; the rest of Demeter's career consisted of 4 games.

Early in their existence, the Mets made a number of misguided trades in their quest for a third baseman. The worst of them were the sacrifice of Amos Otis to the Royals for Joe Foy in December 1969 and the dumping of Nolan Ryan (and three other players) on the Angels for Jim Fregosi. Foy lasted one season in New York and one more elsewhere before retiring, and Fregosi hit .232 in a season and a half at Shea Stadium before playing out the string for six more years. In fourteen seasons with Kansas City, Otis collected more hits, runs, doubles, triples, RBIs, walks, and stolen bases than the Mets' club record holders in those categories; and Ryan became a legend.

In 1971 the Giants managed to acquire and rid themselves of Frank Duffy in two of their worst deals. In May they sent future NL home-run champion George Foster to the Reds for the shortstop; in November they peddled the .232 lifetime hitter to the Indians for Sam McDowell, who had only 19 more victories in his sore arm, and threw in Gaylord Perry, who would win 180 games after he left San Francisco.

THE MILK WAGON

These players kept their bags packed for an entire season.

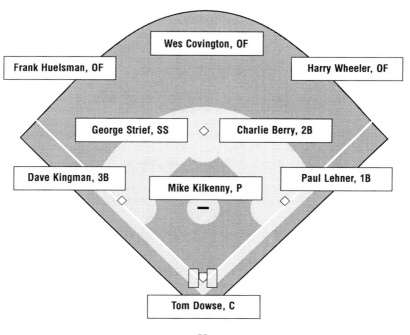

Wes Covington, OF

Frank Huelsman, OF

Harry Wheeler, OF

George Strief, SS

Charlie Berry, 2B

Dave Kingman, 3B

Mike Kilkenny, P

Paul Lehner, 1B

Tom Dowse, C

Lehner toured half of the AL in 1951, playing outfield for the Athletics, White Sox, Browns, and Indians; his .172 average didn't help his lifetime mark of .257; the lefty batter had been a part-time first baseman earlier in his seven-year career.

In 1884, his only season in the majors, Berry hit .224 while bouncing around Union Association (UA) franchises in Altoona, Kansas City, Chicago, and Pittsburgh.

Kingman spent time with the Mets, Padres, Angels, and Yankees in 1977.

Two of Strief's 1884 teams were in the UA: Kansas City and Pittsburgh; he started the season with St. Louis of the AA and ended it with Cleveland of the NL. He hit .189 that year and .207 in his five-year career.

Dave Kingman is the most recent player to wear four different uniforms in a season.

Huelsman saw action with the White Sox, Tigers, Browns, and Senators in 1904, batting .245, just a shade under his three-year career mark of .258.

Covington was a journeyman who hit .279 for eleven seasons, mostly with the Braves and Phillies. His journey had the most stops in 1961, when he wore not only Milwaukee and Philadelphia uniforms but also those of the White Sox and Athletics.

Wheeler had already been around the block a few times by the time he appeared with *five* different clubs in 1884. He had played for five teams in his first five seasons when he embarked on an odyssey that took him to St. Louis (AA), Kansas City (UA), Chicago (UA), Pittsburgh (UA), and Baltimore (UA) before ending his major league career with a .244 mark for the season and .228 overall.

Dowse appeared in NL games with Louisville, Cincinnati, Philadelphia, and Washington in 1892. His average for the year was .165, his three-year career total, .195.

Kilkenny is the most recent pitcher to work for four franchises in a season. In 1972 he won 4 games and lost one, all with the Indians. Before that, he had pitched one game each for the Tigers and A's; afterward, he appeared in 5 games for the Padres. His ERA for the year was 3.78; his career record was 23–18, with a 4.44 ERA.

Honorable mention to pitchers Ted Gray (1955), Willis Hudlin (1940), and Al Atkinson (1884) for anticipating Kilkenny.

STAYING HOME

Even before the advent of free agency, it was rare for a player to spend a lengthy career with one club. These were the players—Hall of Famers all—who stayed the longest with one franchise.

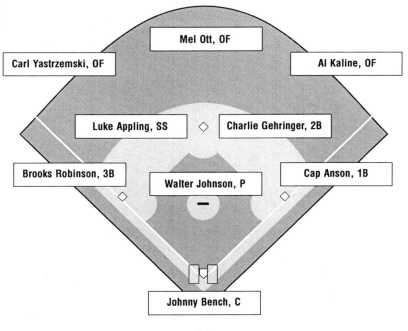

Anson spent twenty-two years (1876–97) with the Cubs, as a playing manager for the last nineteen.

Gehringer's nineteen-year career (1924–42) was with the Tigers.

Robinson established the record for most seasons with one club, twenty-three (1955–77) with the Orioles.

Appling was with the White Sox for twenty seasons beginning in 1930 and ending in 1950 (with 1944 off for military duty).

Yastrzemski tied Robinson's record when he retired from the Red Sox after the 1983 season.

Ott was with the Giants for twenty-two years (1926–47), the final six as player-manager.

Kaline's twenty-two seasons (1953–74) were with the Tigers.

Bench lasted seventeen years (1967–83) with the Reds.

Johnson labored for the Senators for twenty-one years (1907–27).

THE MECHANICAL MAN
DETROIT TIGERS – 2ND BASE   1934

Charlie Gehringer was called the Mechanical Man for his flawless, almost robotlike, defensive skills.

Bill Dickey of the Yankees and Ted Lyons of the White Sox tied Bench and Johnson, respectively, but they played in fewer games.

Among the managers who have only served with one club, Tom Lasorda has put in the most seasons—twenty-one (1976–96) with the Los Angeles Dodgers; the man from whom he inherited the job, Walter Alston, headed the Dodgers for twenty-three years (1954–76), but the first four of those seasons were in Brooklyn.

Honorable mention to Frankie Crosetti, who holds the record for wearing one uniform in the most seasons without every wearing another. In thirty-seven years as a player (1932–46), player-coach (1947–48), and coach (1949–68) for the Yankees, Crosetti picked up a record twenty-three World Series checks.

Even Crosetti's tenure in the Bronx pales before Red Schoendienst's forty-six years (as of Opening Day 1996) spent with the Cardinals as player, coach, and manager. His service, while interrupted by stints with other teams, is the longest in one franchise's uniform and is approaching the half decade that Connie Mack managed the Athletics in mufti.

TRADED LEAGUE LEADERS

Even being traded in the middle of a season did not prevent the following players from leading the league in important categories.

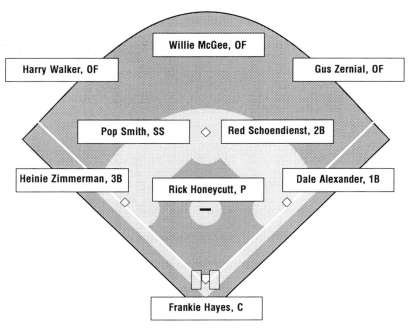

Alexander was the first player to win a batting crown while playing for two teams in the same year. Hitting a mere .250 for the Tigers, he was traded to the Red Sox on June 12, 1932, and proceeded to belt AL pitching at a .372 clip the rest of the way to take the batting title with a .367 mark.

In 1957, Schoendienst led the NL with 200 hits despite being traded from the Giants to the Braves on June 15.

Zimmerman led the NL with 83 RBIs playing for the Cubs (until August 28) and Giants in 1916.

Smith, with Pittsburgh and Boston in 1889, led the NL by striking out 68 times.

Walker matched Alexander's feat, in the NL in 1947. The Cardinals let him go to the Phillies 10 games into the season. While he batted only .200 for St. Louis, he recorded a .371 mark for Philadelphia to win the crown with an overall .363 average.

In 1951, Zernial not only matched Zimmerman's accomplishment, taking AL RBI honors with 129, but also led the league in homers, with 33. He did most of his damage to AL pitching for the Athletics, following his move from the White Sox after only 4 games.

HEINIE ZIMMERMAN
CHICAGO CUBS – 3RD BASE 1912

Heinie Zimmerman is the only twentieth-century player to win a Triple Crown but fail to gain entry to the Hall of Fame.

McGee sat on his league-leading .335 average for the Cardinals after switching leagues, to the A's, in late August 1990; he hit only .274 in 29 games for Oakland.

Hayes participated in the most double plays by a catcher in 1945 while splitting the season between the Athletics and Indians.

Like McGee, Honeycutt switched leagues, from the Rangers to the Dodgers in August 1983, and so was something of a bystander during the final weeks of his ERA crown (2.42); he must have had one eye on AL rivals during his time with Los Angeles because he was pounded for 5.77 earned runs per 9 innings in nine appearances.

Honorable mention to John Anderson (1898, Brooklyn and Washington) for leading the NL in both slugging and triples, Roy Cullenbine (1945, Indians and Tigers) for walking the most times in the AL, and Red Barrett (1945, Braves and Cardinals) for winning the most games in the NL.

BEST INTERESTS

The first baseball official to invoke "the best interests of baseball" was UA secretary William Warren White, when he committed the new league to that standard in a letter to the *New York Clipper* in 1884. Since then, the expression has become a mantra available to league presidents and commissioners as justification to prevent what they don't like. The following were victims of the incantation.

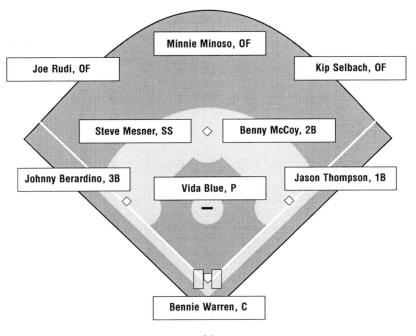

Commissioner Bowie Kuhn detected irregularities in a planned three-way deal among the Pirates, Yankees, and Angels in 1981 and said no to Thompson's going to New York for Jim Spencer.

Commissioner Landis ruled in 1943 that the Tigers had been keeping McCoy in their farm system illegally and so had no right to exchange him for Wally Moses of the Athletics. As part of the ruling, McCoy became a free agent and signed with the Athletics.

Berardino got Commissioner Happy Chandler to cancel his 1947 trade from the Browns to the Senators for Gerry Priddy by saying he was going to retire to become an actor; as soon as the deal was scratched, Berardino unretired himself to go off to Cleveland, where Bill Veeck's blandishments included a screen test with some of his Hollywood friends. After dropping the second "r" in his name, the utility infielder went on to a thirty-year stretch as Dr. Steve Hardy on the daytime soap opera *General Hospital*.

Landis killed the sales of Mesner, by Cincinnati in 1943, and Warren, by Philadelphia in 1942, because their prospective buyers in Brooklyn and Pittsburgh, respectively, were unaware that the players had been drafted into the armed services.

Forced by a commissioner's ruling to stay in Pittsburgh, Jason Thompson became the Pirates' first baseman for five seasons.

In 1976, Kuhn nixed the intention of Oakland's Charlie Finley to sell Rudi to the Red Sox and Blue to the Yankees for $1 million each. Rudi escaped as a free agent, and Blue later went to the Giants for seven players and somewhat less money.

Commissioner Fay Vincent scotched the White Sox's planned reactivation of Minoso in 1990 on the grounds that it amounted to nothing more than a publicity stunt to make the sixty-seven-year-old baseball's only player to appear in games in six decades.

After suspending the talented Selbach for inert play with the last-place Senators in 1904, AL president Ban Johnson encouraged his trade to Boston so that the outfielder could flourish and the fledgling league would look more competitive against the NL.

BOTH LEAGUES

Frank Robinson was the first black manager in both the National and American leagues, but that is only one of his accomplishments in both circuits. Trivia experts will know what these players succeeded in doing in both major leagues.

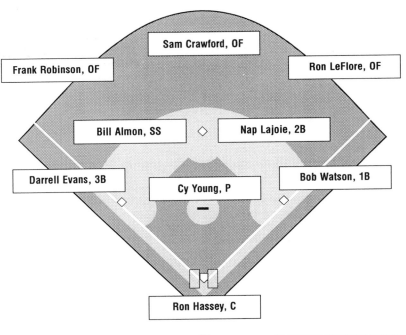

Sam Crawford, OF

Frank Robinson, OF

Ron LeFlore, OF

Bill Almon, SS

Nap Lajoie, 2B

Darrell Evans, 3B

Cy Young, P

Bob Watson, 1B

Ron Hassey, C

Watson is the only player to hit for the cycle in both leagues; he turned the trick with both the 1977 Astros and the 1979 Red Sox.

Only Lajoie has headed both loops in RBIs; he led NL batters for the 1898 Phillies and topped the AL for the 1901 Athletics and the 1904 Indians.

Evans is the only one to belt 40 homers in a season in each league; he reached that mark for the 1973 Braves and the 1985 Tigers.

On a negative note, Almon led both leagues in errors (with the Padres in 1977 and the White Sox in 1982, when he tied with Toronto's Alfredo Griffin).

Robinson is the only player to earn an MVP Award in each league (1961 Reds and 1966 Orioles). He also topped both circuits in slugging (1960–62 Reds and 1966 Orioles) and in runs scored (1956 and 1962 Reds and 1966 Orioles).

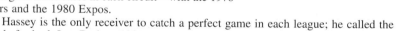

NAP LAJOIE
PHILADELPHIA ATHLETICS – 2ND BASE   1915

When Nap Lajoie jumped from the Phillies to the Athletics in 1901, he gave the fledgling American League instant credibility.

In the pre-Ruth era, Crawford led each league in both homers (1901 Reds and 1908 Tigers) and triples (1902 Reds and five times with the Tigers).

LeFlore is the only one who can lay claim to stealing the most bases in each circuit—with the 1978 Tigers and the 1980 Expos.

Hassey is the only receiver to catch a perfect game in each league; he called the signals for both Len Barker (1981 Indians) and Dennis Martinez (1991 Expos).

Young pitched three no-hitters (for the Cleveland Spiders in 1897 and a perfect game in 1904 and another no-hitter in 1908 for the Red Sox), posted more than 200 victories, struck out more than 1,000 batters, and topped all hurlers in one season or another in wins, winning percentage, ERA, and strikeouts in both the NL and the AL.

Honorable mentions: Only Ed Delahanty has led both leagues in batting. Like Crawford, Buck Freeman topped both loops in homers, and Brett Butler led both in triples. Jim Bunning, Nolan Ryan, and Dennis Martinez matched Young's 1,000 strikeouts in each loop; the first two also hurled an NL and an AL no-hitter.

Sparky Anderson is the only manager to win 100 games in a season and to earn a World Series title for each league (1975 and 1976 Reds and 1984 Tigers).

YOUNGEST PLAYERS

The youngest players to appear in a major league game are:

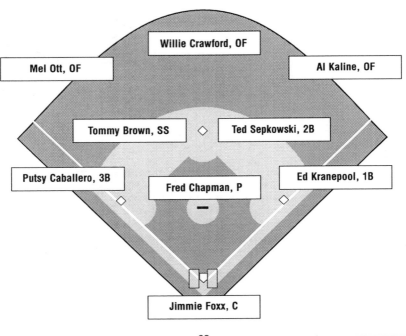

Sepkowski and Kaline were eighteen years old when they made their respective debuts, with the Indians in 1942 and the Tigers in 1953.

Kranepool (1962 Mets), Ott (1926 Giants), Crawford (1964 Dodgers), and Foxx (1925 Athletics) were all seventeen.

Caballero got his chance with the Phillies and Brown his with the Dodgers at age sixteen because in 1944 so many draft-age players were in the army.

Chapman, four months shy of his fifteenth birthday on July 22, 1887, was the youngest player ever to appear in a major league game. As the starting pitcher for the AA Philadelphia club, he lasted into the fifth inning, when, despite holding a 6–4 lead, the Cleveland players protested a play at the plate so vigorously that the umpire declared a forfeit for Philadelphia. Chapman was, however, denied the victory. He never appeared in another big league game.

The second-youngest player was Joe Nuxhall, who entered a game for the Reds on June 10, 1944, when he was still more than six weeks away from his sixteenth birthday. In two-thirds of an inning, the lefty surrendered 2 hits and 5 walks, ending his first

No player without a Cooperstown plaque had an exclusive engagement with one club longer than Ed Kranepool's 18 seasons with the Mets.

game—and his first season—with a 67.50 ERA. Nuxhall returned to the big leagues in 1952, compiling a 135–117 record over the next fifteen seasons.

The youngest pitcher to start a twentieth-century game was Jim Derrington, of the 1956 White Sox. He lost the game, but two months shy of seventeen, he was the youngest American Leaguer to get a hit. He was, however, washed up at eighteen.

The youngest player to appear in 100 games was Robin Yount, the Brewers' regular shortstop in 1974, who did not turn nineteen until that September.

The youngest manager was Roger Peckinpaugh, who took over the New York Yankees on September 16, 1914, at the preposterous age of twenty-three years, seven months, and eleven days. He survived only through the final few weeks of the season. The youngest full-season pilot was Lou Boudreau of the Indians, who was four months past his twenty-fourth birthday when he began his first season as dugout boss in 1942.

BEST ROOKIE YEARS

In 1987, Mark McGwire hit 49 homers (a rookie record) and drove in 118 runs. Impressive, but he can't make this team.

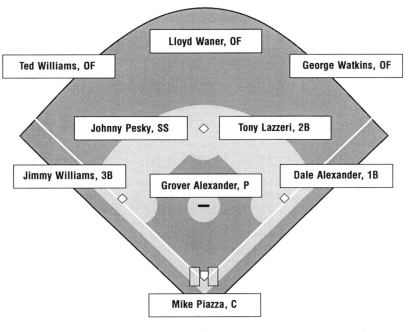

Lloyd Waner, OF

Ted Williams, OF

George Watkins, OF

Johnny Pesky, SS

Tony Lazzeri, 2B

Jimmy Williams, 3B

Grover Alexander, P

Dale Alexander, 1B

Mike Piazza, C

Dale Alexander hit .343 with 43 doubles and 25 home runs among his AL-leading 215 hits; he also drove in 137 runs for the 1929 Tigers.

Lazzeri debuted with the Yankees in 1926 by batting .275, slugging 18 homers, and driving in 114 runs.

Jimmy Williams had a career year in his initial season, 1899, with the Pirates, hitting .355, reaching personal highs of 116 RBIs and 126 runs scored, and leading the NL with 27 triples (a rookie record).

Pesky's .331 batting average with the 1942 Red Sox was built on an AL-leading 205 base hits.

Waner's 223 base hits (a record for first-year players) translated into a .355 batting average for the 1927 Pirates.

Watkins never again came within sixty points of his .373 rookie-record average for the 1930 Cardinals.

Ted Williams gave AL pitchers early warning of what was to come with a .327 average, 44 doubles, 31 homers, and a first-year record (and league-leading) 145 RBIs for the 1939 Red Sox.

Piazza broke in with the Dodgers in 1993 by hitting .318, stroking 35 homers, and driving in 112 runs.

GEORGE WATKINS
NEW YORK GIANTS – OUTFIELD   1934

Buried for years in the talent-deep St. Louis farm system, George Watkins was thirty years old when he completed his record-setting rookie year in 1930.

Grover Alexander (1911 Phillies) holds the rookie records for victories (28), complete games (31), and shutouts (7); the righthander led the NL in all three categories in his first season.

Aside from first-year home-run record holder McGwire, honorable mentions to Tony Oliva (1964 Twins), the only rookie batting titlist; Fred Lynn (1975 Red Sox), the only rookie to win the Most Valuable Player Award; and Dwight Gooden (1984 Mets), whose 276 strikeouts is a rookie record.

Only three managers (Bucky Harris, 1924 Senators; Eddie Dyer, 1946 Cardinals; and Ralph Houk, 1961 Yankees) have won a World Series in their managerial debuts.

BEST DEBUTS

Talk about getting off to a good start.

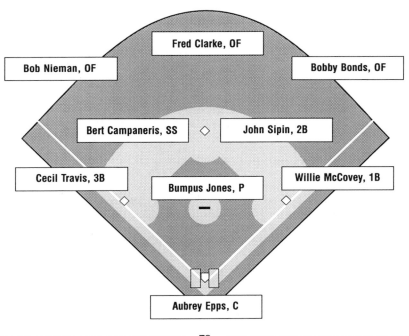

Fred Clarke, OF

Bob Nieman, OF

Bobby Bonds, OF

Bert Campaneris, SS

John Sipin, 2B

Cecil Travis, 3B

Bumpus Jones, P

Willie McCovey, 1B

Aubrey Epps, C

McCovey began his Hall of Fame career by banging out a record 2 triples and adding 2 singles for the 1959 Giants.

Like McCovey, Sipin had a pair of three-base hits; unlike McCovey, the infielder (for the 1969 Padres) never hit another one and never made it to his sophomore season.

Travis had a record 5 hits (all singles) in a twelve-inning contest for the 1933 Senators.

Campaneris (1964 Athletics) is one of only three players to knock 2 round-trippers in his maiden game.

Nieman (1951 Browns) went Campaneris one better by homering in his first 2 major league at-bats.

Clarke matched Travis's 5 hits (4 singles and a triple) for Louisville in 1894, accomplishing the feat in a 9-inning regulation game.

Bonds (1968 Giants) is one of only two players to hit a grand slam in his first major league appearance. (The other was pitcher Bill Duggleby of the 1898 Phillies.)

In 1959, Willie McCovey won the Rookie of the Year award for his .354 batting average, despite appearing in only 52 games.

Epps collected a triple and 2 singles in 4 at-bats and drove in 3 runs for the 1933 Pirates—and never played another big league game.

Most amazing of all was Jones, who, pitching for the Reds on the last day of the 1892 season, became the only hurler to post a no-hitter in his first game, against the Pirates. The following year, unable to adjust to the new pitching distance of sixty feet six inches, he was batted around for a 10.19 ERA and won only one game while losing 4 before disappearing from the major leagues. Bobo Holloman (1953 St. Louis Browns) and Ted Breitenstein (1891 AA St. Louis Browns) pitched no-hitters in their first starts but not their first games.

Honorable mention to third-baseman Charlie Reilly, the first player to hit 2 homers in his first big league game, for Columbus of the AA in 1889.

Joining McCovey and Sipin as the only other players to triple twice in their initial games are Roy Weatherly of the 1936 Indians and Ed Irvin of the 1912 Tigers.

ONCE WAS ENOUGH

The oddest of rookies are that small group—fewer than forty—who played in more than half of their teams' games and then disappeared from the major league ranks. The following played the most games.

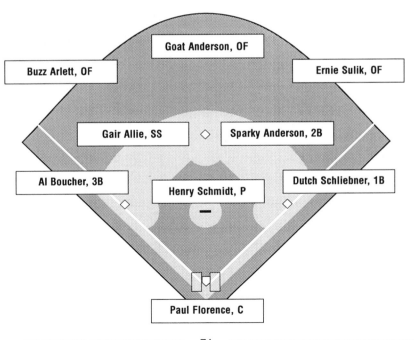

When it became clear that an infection in his optic nerves would keep George Sisler out of the lineup for the entire 1923 season and that no one on hand would be an adequate replacement, the Browns went out and acquired Schliebner from the Dodgers. The righty swinger went on to hit .275 for St. Louis (.271 over-all) in 127 games (146 for the two clubs combined), but that was hardly good enough to keep him around after Sisler returned the following year.

Sparky Anderson, of course, has had a much longer major league career as a manager, with the Reds and Tigers, than as an infielder. As the Phillies' second baseman in 1959, his single big league season, the longtime defensive whiz in the Dodgers' farm system posted an anemic .218 batting average and a paltry .249 slugging percentage in 152 games. Having replaced one second baseman with a pretty good bat, Solly Hemus (the regular in 1958), he was, in turn, replaced by another, Tony Taylor (who took over in 1960).

Sparky Anderson's 2,194 victories as a manager rank third on the all-time list after Connie Mack and John McGraw.

It is not surprising that Boucher, despite his .231 average, lasted 147 games with the Federal League (FL) St. Louis Terriers in 1914. The Feds were, after all, a third major league that created a passel of new big league jobs. It is equally unsurprising that he was discarded the next season after the Terriers signed Bobby Vaughn, whose .280 average helped boost the team from last place to second.

Allie appeared in 121 games—95 of them at shortstop—for the 1954 Pirates. His .199 batting average and 84 strikeouts made it abundantly clear that he was overmatched at the major league level; when Dick Groat became available for full-time duty in 1955, Allie became an ex–major leaguer.

The least likely member of this team, Arlett hit .313, including 26 doubles and 18 homers, in 121 games (94 as an outfielder) for the 1931 Phillies. On the other hand, the switch hitter had earned a reputation for ineptitude in the field during his thirteen years with the PCL Oakland Oaks leading up to his rookie season. He stayed around in the high minors until 1937, compiling a lifetime average of .341 and slugging 432 homers. However, he was barely missed in Philadelphia, for rookie Kiddo Davis (.309) and newcomer Hal Lee (.303, 42 doubles, 18 homers) joined Hall of Famer Chuck Klein in the outfield in 1932.

By way of contrast, Goat Anderson managed only a .207 average with a mere 5 extra-base hits (for a nearly invisible .225 slugging average) in his tenure with the 1907 Pirates. His 80 walks (in 127 games, 117 in the outfield) did, however, help him steal 27 bases and score 73 runs. He replaced Bob Ganley (.258 in 1906) and was succeeded by Owen Wilson (.227 in 1908); in 1912, Wilson would belt a record 36 triples.

Sulik was the fourth outfielder for the 1936 Phillies. He appeared in 122 contests (105 in the outfield) and hit an acceptable .287; the lowest average among the frontline outfielders was Lou Chiozza's .297, and the team as a whole batted .281. The lefty hitter became expendable with the acquisition of Hersh Martin (.283 in 1937) and Earl Browne (.292) and the maturation of Morrie Arnovich (.290) to patrol the pasture with Chuck Klein and Joe Moore.

The 1926 Giants had six future Hall of Famers on their roster, but Florence, whose 76 games behind the plate were the most on the team, wasn't one of them. He was in the lineup as often as he was only because veteran Frank Snyder was too old for anything but backup duty. Florence's .229 average and league-leading 17 errors persuaded manager John McGraw to dump both his receivers and acquire the more steady, if unspectacular, Zack Taylor and Al DeVormer the following season.

Native Texan Schmidt posted a 21–13 record for the 1903 Dodgers before deciding that he was so uncomfortable living in the Northeast that he was retiring and going home. The righthander is the only twentieth-century pitcher to win 20 games in his only major league season. John Cronin, his replacement in the rotation, won 12 and lost 23 in 1904.

This squad even gets a manager—Harry Wright, who managed Providence to the NL pennant in his only season as a major league pilot (1879)—and a general manager—Stan Musial, who accomplished the same feat in his only year of presiding over a big league front office (1967, with the Cardinals).

Most of the one-season big leaguers saw their brief action in seasons when there were three major leagues (1884, 1890, and 1914–15) or during World War II. Two of those who deserve honorable mention are:

Harry Sage, who appeared behind the plate in 80 (of his 81) games for the 1890 Toledo Maumees (AA), the most ever for a one-year receiver; however, his minuscule .149 average prevented him from having a longer career.

Bob Maier, the only one-year big leaguer to play for a world championship team.

While the third baseman's .263 average helped the Tigers stay in the 1945 pennant race, it wasn't good enough to keep him in the lineup every day after Hank Greenberg's release from the military. With the return of the future Hall of Famer to Detroit, Maier had to share playing time with Jimmy Outlaw, who was moved to third to make room for Greenberg in the outfield. With Outlaw starting at third in every game of the World Series against the Cubs, Maier singled in his only plate appearance, as a pinch hitter. The following season, Maier and Outlaw lost the hot-corner job to another future Hall of Famer, George Kell.

Other notable one-season performers:

After 58 games of the 1901 season, first baseman Burt Hart was batting .311 for the Baltimore Orioles when he slugged umpire John Haskell after being called out after trying to stretch a double into a triple. AL president Ban Johnson banned the promising rookie for life.

Outfielder Tex Vache led the AL with 49 pinch at-bats for the 1925 Red Sox. While he collected only 10 hits in that role, he did bat .340 in 53 games as an outfielder.

Scotty Ingerton was a supersub for the 1911 Braves, breaking into the lineup at every infield and outfield position. He also hit a respectable .250 in 136 games.

Bill Wakefield appeared in 62 games (58 of them in relief) for the 1964 Mets, the record for one-season pitchers. The righthander compiled a 3–5 record, with a 3.61 ERA.

THEY DIED WITH THEIR SPIKES ON

Although Lou Gehrig has been the most noted player forced to the sidelines by a fatal illness, he was out of the game two years before succumbing to the disease that bears his name. The following met quicker ends.

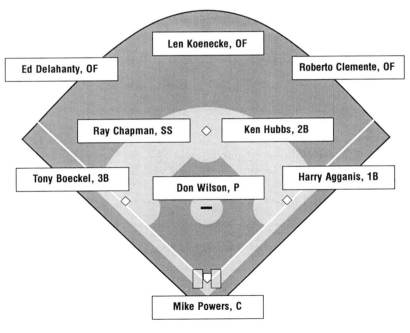

Len Koenecke, OF

Ed Delahanty, OF

Roberto Clemente, OF

Ray Chapman, SS

Ken Hubbs, 2B

Tony Boeckel, 3B

Harry Agganis, 1B

Don Wilson, P

Mike Powers, C

Local favorite Agganis had been an all-American quarterback at Boston University and was a big part of the Red Sox' plans for the future when he was felled, on June 27, 1955, at age twenty-five, by a pulmonary embolism brought on by a bout of pneumonia. He hit .251 with 11 homers in 1954 and .313 through only 25 games in 1955.

The 1962 National League Rookie of the Year, Hubbs set records for most at-bats, most consecutive errorless games, and most consecutive chances without a misplay (all since surpassed) while on his way to becoming the first rookie to win a Gold Glove Award; he also hit .260 for the Cubs. After a somewhat less spectacular sophomore season, he died, on February 15, 1964, when the private plane he was flying crashed in Utah. He was twenty-two years old.

Boeckel was a thirty-one-year-old, six-season veteran when he was hit by a car on February 16, 1924, near Torrey Pines, California, while gazing at the wreckage of an automobile collision he had sur-

Roberto Clemente is the only player since Lou Gehrig to be exempted from Cooperstown's five-year waiting period after playing his last game.

vived just minutes before. The career .282 hitter had batted as high as .313, for the 1921 Braves.

On August 16, 1920, Chapman took a pitch by Yankee hurler Carl Mays in the left temple, was carried from the field to a hospital, and died some hours later, the only beaning fatality in major league history. A nine-year veteran with the Indians, Chapman was hitting .303 (.278 lifetime) at the time of the accident, which resulted from a combination of the late-afternoon sun at the Polo Grounds, Mays's unorthodox underhand delivery, and Chapman's crouched-over-the-plate stance. Numerous lunatics threatened Mays's safety the next time he came to Ohio, but manager Tris Speaker distracted Clevelanders by rallying the team and, with Joe Sewell filling in at short at the beginning of his Hall of Fame career, led the Indians on a successful stretch run to a pennant.

The circumstances surrounding Delahanty's death remain an enigma. One of a record five brothers to reach the big leagues, Delahanty had already established his Hall of Fame credentials (a .346 career batting average, including three .400 seasons) when he was suspended by the Washington Senators in 1903 for excessive drinking. The righty slugger boarded a train in Detroit, drank all the way to Buffalo, got tossed off the train by a conductor, tangled with a bridge watchman, and died—whether by accident, suicide, or homicide is unclear—when he fell from the International Bridge into the Niagara River on July 2. A sizable insurance policy he took out just before his death, with his daughter as beneficiary, fueled speculation that his death was a suicide.

Whereas Delahanty's death was mysterious, Koenecke's was bizarre. After hitting .320 for the Dodgers in 1934 and getting off to an equally good start the following year, the lefty hitter began to irritate manager Casey Stengel by wandering absentmindedly off first base and getting tagged out and jogging out to the wrong position. On September 17 the dugout boss ordered the outfielder back to Brooklyn from St. Louis. But Koenecke got off the train in Detroit, chartered a plane to Buffalo, attempted to take over the aircraft in mid-flight, and was killed by two blows to the head from a fire extinguisher wielded by the pilot. Stengel never mentioned the incident without expressing regret that he had failed to recognize the symptoms of Koenecke's acute mental illness.

On New Year's Eve a few months after collecting his 3,000th hit on the final day of the 1972 season, Clemente died when his plane, carrying food and supplies to victims of an earthquake in Nicaragua, crashed taking off from San Juan, Puerto Rico. The circumstances of his death convinced the Hall of Fame to waive its five-year eligibility requirement and recognize Clemente's accomplishments over an eighteen-year career with the Pirates by inducting him immediately.

On April 12, 1909, during the first game played at Shibe Park, Powers became the first victim of an on-field fatal accident when he crashed into a wall while chasing a seventh-inning pop foul. Even though he completed the game, the receiver was taken to the hospital afterward and operated on to stanch internal bleeding. He died two weeks later when, after two additional operations, gangrene attacked his bowels. A backup catcher for most of his eleven-year career, the lifetime .216 hitter was in the lineup for the ballpark inaugural only because he was starting-pitcher Eddie Plank's personal receiver.

Wilson had won 104 games—two of them no-hitters—in nine seasons with the Astros when he asphyxiated himself in his own garage on January 5, 1975.

The prototypical athlete dying young was James Creighton of the Brooklyn Excelsiors in the early 1860s. Often cited as the first hurler to snap his wrist in delivering the ball, he was also a prodigious slugger. He died at the age of twenty-one, on October 18, 1862, four days after blasting a ball beyond the outfielders for an inside-the-park home run—with a swing that, as was customary at the time, relied more on upper-body motion than wrist action—in a game against the Union Club of Morrisania. He collapsed as he rounded first but managed to circle the bases even though he was in obvious pain. It was later learned that he had ruptured his bladder with the force of his final swing.

Baseball's most famous suicide was Willard Hershberger of the Reds, who severed his jugular vein with a razor in a Boston hotel room on August 3, 1940. Many commentators have attributed the backup catcher's act to depression over having called for a pitch to Giants' catcher Harry Danning a few days earlier that ended up as a grand slam and a Cincinnati defeat in a key game. What is not commonly known is that Hershberger had indicated to Reds' manager Bill McKechnie that he planned to take his own life. At the time, the pilot had regarded the threat as a passing glumness; thereafter, he never spoke of the incident.

The only suicide among active pilots was Chick Stahl of the Red Sox. After becoming player-manager near the end of the 1906 season, Stahl swallowed a lethal dose of carbolic acid during spring training the following year. The reason he gave— "Boys, I couldn't help it; it drove me to it"—remained an enigma until 1986, when a Boston magazine uncovered the extent of the outfielder's stress over his womanizing. It seems that after marrying in November 1906, he discovered that a second woman was carrying his child. In addition, a third woman had twice tried to shoot him for having deserted her.

Harry Pulliam is the only league president to die by his own hand. On July 28, 1909, the NL executive blew his brains out in the New York Athletic Club; he was driven to the act at least in part by New York manager John McGraw's unrelenting criticism of Pulliam's decision to rule against the Giants in the Merkle Boner game.

THE EXILES

Baseball has had to admit to more dirty laundry than just the 1919 Black Sox.

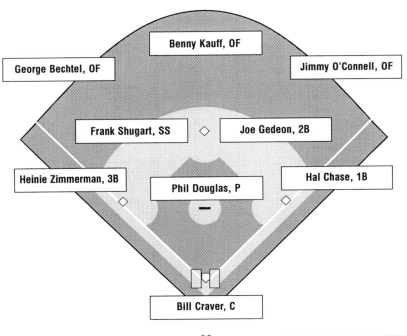

Known as Prince Hal for his fancy glovework, Chase was baseball's most accomplished crook. His technique was the timely misplay disguised by an ability to make miscues look as if they were someone else's fault. As early as his fourth season (1908) he was being accused of throwing games for profit by Yankee manager George Stallings, an accusation echoed by Stallings's eventual successor, Frank Chance, five years later. For all his dishonesty, Chase managed to dodge bullets for fifteen seasons by batting .291 (including a NL-leading .339 in 1916) and perfecting such plays as the 3–6–3 double play. His closest call came in 1918 when Reds' manager Christy Mathewson suspended him for a succession of marginally errant tosses to pitchers covering first base. Chase was exonerated at a postseason hearing, however, primarily because Mathewson was in France with the American Expeditionary Forces and couldn't testify. Chase's later

Hal Chase, baseball's Prince of Darkness.

involvement in the Black Sox scandal has been obscured by his escape from punishment, even though his name popped up regularly in the 1920 grand jury hearings that led to the indictment of the Chicago Eight, including testimony that he had won $40,000 betting on Cincinnati. Curiously, when he inquired of Commissioner Landis about his status in organized baseball, the sport's chief executive wrote him a letter stating that there were no charges—either pending or contemplated—against him. As a result, despite all his baggage, Chase was never formally expelled from the game by any authority. By 1920, however, he was an untouchable as far as all sixteen major league teams were concerned; his fate amounted to a de facto banishment. He later became part of a crooked ring that controlled five of the eight teams in the PCL and ended up playing out the string in California outlaw leagues and semipro circuits in Arizona mining towns.

Gedeon became the "ninth man out" in the Black Sox scandal when Commissioner Landis banned him for "guilty knowledge" of the plot because he had attended meetings with gamblers to discuss the conspiracy. On the field, Gedeon was a .244 hitter over seven seasons with the Senators, Yankees, and Browns.

Zimmerman was Chase's coconspirator with the Giants in 1919 when the pair approached outfielder Benny Kauff with a $500 bribe to help throw a game. The third baseman also stood accused of offering pitcher Fred Toney a similar proposition. Manager John McGraw got rid of both culprits by first suspending them, then offering them 1920 salaries so ridiculously low that they refused to sign, even though the reserve clause prohibited them from doing so with any other club. Zimmerman, a lifetime .295 hitter in thirteen NL seasons, is the only Triple Crown winner (in 1912, with the Cubs) without a Cooperstown plaque. He is otherwise best known for his futile pursuit of Eddie Collins down the third-base line as the White Sox' second baseman scored a key run in the sixth game of the 1917 World Series because no one was covering the plate.

Shugart became a victim of AL president Ban Johnson's insistence on decorum after he punched out umpire John Haskell and caused a riot that required police intervention on August 28, 1901. An eight-year major league veteran with a .267 career average, the White Sox' shortstop had been part of worse melees in the NL, but Johnson, intolerant of all such rowdiness in his circuit, suspended the infielder for life, even though the ban ruptured the relationship between the league president and Chicago owner Charles Comiskey.

Despite his denial of accusations that he offered teammate Jim Devlin a $500 bribe to throw a game and even though there was evidence to support his innocence, Bechtel was suspended by the Louisville Grays in 1876—on a trumped-up charge of drunkenness rather than for dishonesty. After the following season, the NL made the punishment permanent, along with those of the so-called Louisville Crooks (including Devlin). The outfielder was hitting .200 at the time of his alleged crime.

Kauff's punishment came not for anything he did in collusion with Zimmerman or Chase but, rather, as a result of an arbitrary judgment by Landis following the outfielder's 1920 indictment for employing a used-car business he owned with his brother as a cover for an auto theft ring. Landis banned Kauff before his trial began and refused to relent even after the outfielder was acquitted and despite character references given by John McGraw and NL president John Tener. The lefty-swinging Kauff had won both FL batting crowns (1914 and 1915) and was a steady, if unspectacular, performer for the Giants until his arrest.

A reserve outfielder for the Giants in 1923 and 1924, O'Connell precipitated major league baseball's last game-fixing scandal when he offered Philadelphia shortstop Heinie Sand a $500 bribe to let up in a key series. Summoned by Landis to explain his actions, the outfielder claimed he had been put up to the move by coach Cozy Dolan and several better-known teammates. Landis outlawed O'Connell and Dolan but exonerated the others. The lefty hitter had compiled a .270 career mark before his banishment.

Craver was one of the four Louisville Crooks banned for life by the NL after the 1877 season. The other three either confessed or failed to defend themselves against charges that they had thrown either exhibition games against non-NL teams or contests against Cincinnati that cost Louisville the pennant. Craver, on the other hand, admitted to nothing except late-night carousing. Nevertheless, he suffered the same fate as his teammates partly because of accusations (later recanted) by other players that he had rattled them into making errors and partly because he refused to allow team officials to read his private telegrams. Craver, a .244 lifetime hitter in the NL, was the regular shortstop for Louisville in 1877 but had been a catcher for much of a career that saw him implicated in several earlier gambling scandals.

In August 1922, Douglas, fed up with manager John McGraw's tirades, went out and got tanked, then made the mistake of writing a letter to St. Louis outfielder Les Mann suggesting that he was ready to "go fishing" for the rest of the season if the Cardinals made it worth his while. His letter ended up in the hands of Landis, who banished him. In nine seasons, the righthander compiled a 93-93 record; at the time of his indiscretion he was 11–4, with what turned out to be an NL-leading 2.63 ERA.

The breadth of baseball's criminal taint is evident from the number of the following who exited the sport because of their association with gamblers.

Two managers: Jack O'Connor of the 1910 Browns, who issued orders to third baseman Red Corriden to play deep against Nap Lajoie in a season-ending doubleheader, wasn't interested in gambling; he got himself banished for trying to throw the batting championship to the Cleveland second baseman at the expense of Ty Cobb. The expulsion of all-time hit leader and Cincinnati pilot Pete Rose in 1989, on the other hand, had everything to do with his compulsive gambling, even though the official proclamation banning him made no mention of his alleged betting either on Reds' games or on baseball contests in general.

Two coaches: While manager O'Connor was aligning his defense to help Lajoie, Harry Howell was bribing the official scorer to change one of the Cleveland second baseman's at-bats from an error to a hit; he suffered the same fate as his boss. When Jimmy O'Connell implicated Cozy Dolan in the plot to bribe Phillies' shortstop Heinie Sand, the Giants' coach could come up with no better defense than an inability to remember whether he had encouraged the outfielder to approach Sand; he was expelled from baseball along with O'Connell.

A team president: The Phillies' Horace Fogel found himself out of baseball permanently for one too many unsubstantiated accusations that the Giants had won the 1912 pennant because St. Louis manager Roger Bresnahan had not played his best team against his former teammates and because NL umpires favored the New Yorkers.

An owner: William Cox, also of the Phillies, got trapped by Commissioner Landis's strictures against any form of gambling when he admitted, in 1943, to making "some small sentimental bets" on his own team; he was forced to sell his interests in the club within the year.

An umpire: Dick Higham was banished by the NL in 1882 after a handwriting expert proved that he was the author of letters indicating collusion to fix games for the benefit of gamblers.

Even a team physician: Joseph Creamer, a prominent New York physician who also served as the Giants' team doctor, was banned from baseball after umpire Bill Klem accused him of offering a $3,000 bribe to "call close plays the Giants' way" in the makeup contest between New York and Chicago to decide the 1908 pennant in the wake of the Merkle Boner game.

And two entire franchises: Both the New York Mutuals and the Philadelphia Athletics were dumped from the NL for refusing to make their last road trips of the 1876 season; the senior circuit played with only six teams the following year.

Dishonorable mentions to:

Seven of the eight Black Sox: first baseman Chick Gandil, shortstop Swede Risberg, utility infielder Fred McMullin, outfielders Joe Jackson and Happy Felsch, and pitchers Eddie Cicotte and Lefty Williams. But not third baseman Buck Weaver, who had played no part in the plot.

The other three Louisville Crooks: pitcher Jim Devlin, outfielder George Hall, and utilityman Al Nichols.

First baseman Burt Hart, who suffered the same fate as Shugart, at the same hands and for the same reason.

Second baseman Lee Magee, Chase's partner in a poorly executed scheme to throw a 1918 game while the pair played for the Reds. Cincinnati not only won the game, with Magee scoring the winning run, but the plot was exposed when Magee stopped payment on a $500 check he had given a gambler as a "good faith" ante to be wagered on the fixed game. The check ended up in NL president John Heydler's hands, and Chase and Magee ended up answering charges; while the former walked away from the hearing unscathed, at least for a while, the latter was exiled.

First baseman Gene Paulette, who accepted a loan from a gambler involved in the Black Sox scandal and never repaid it. When a letter from Paulette to the gambler indicating the player's willingness to fix games turned up on Landis's desk, the commissioner doled out to Paulette the same fate he had imposed on the Chicago Eight two weeks earlier.

THE REPRIEVED

Others who were accused of misdeeds fared better.

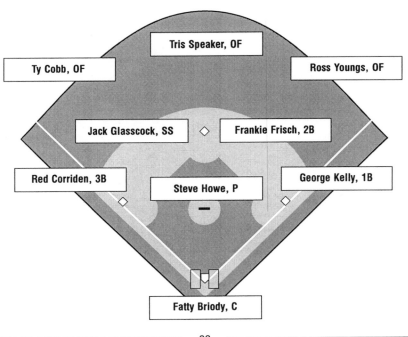

Kelly, Frisch, and Youngs were the three teammates named by Jimmy O'Connell as the instigators of the bribe he offered Heinie Sand. The trio of future Hall of Famers denied any knowledge of the incident and were cleared by Commissioner Landis after a perfunctory investigation.

Corriden was the unwitting instrument of St. Louis manager Jack O'Connor's crude efforts to deny the 1910 batting championship to Ty Cobb and give it to Nap Lajoie. AL president Ban Johnson decided the third baseman was nothing more than a naive rookie following orders and cleared his name. He went on to hit .205 in a five-year career.

While earlier players had disregarded the reserve clause, Glasscock and Briody were the first to jump their contracts in the middle of a season. Members of the NL's Cleveland club in 1884, the pair, along with pitcher Jim McCormick, bolted in August to play for Cincinnati of the UA. The shortstop explained that he had "played long enough for glory," while the catcher called his action "a matter of dollars and cents." The trio helped the Outlaw Reds make a stretch run for the pennant, with Glasscock hitting .419 and Briody con-

FRANKIE FRISCH

Frankie Frisch lasted longer in the big leagues than the others implicated in the O'Connell scandal; his playing career didn't end until 1937, and, as late as 1951, he was a pilot at the major league level.

tributing a .337 average to their new club. Despite its formal blacklisting of contract jumpers, the NL commuted their sentences after the UA folded and settled for fining them. NL president A. G. Mills was so perturbed by this leniency that he refused to run for reelection. Glasscock played until 1895, retiring with a .290 average; Briody lasted only through 1888 and ended with a lifetime .228 mark.

In 1926, Cobb and Speaker, then player-managers of the Tigers and Indians, respectively, were accused by former Detroit pitcher Dutch Leonard of conspiring with him and Cleveland outfielder Joe Wood to fix a September 1919 game to assure the Tigers a third-place finish. The southpaw produced two letters—one written by Wood, the other by Cobb—that substantiated Cobb's wager on the game and heavily implied a fix. As a result, the two player-managers resigned under pressure from AL president Johnson. Landis then entered the drama to rule that Leonard's accusations were lies designed to get even with Cobb for releasing him in 1925 and with Speaker for subsequently refusing to give him a tryout. With Cobb charging that the whole affair was a ploy by Detroit owner Frank Navin to get out from under the star's lucrative contract and with threats of lawsuits flying in all directions, the commissioner prevailed upon the pair to reject offers from the NL and to sign with the Athletics (Cobb) and Senators (Speaker). Both outfielders were eventually enshrined in Cooperstown.

Despite holding unacknowledged baseball records for most suspensions (seven) and most permanent suspensions (two), Howe managed to continue his career. The lefthander's problems stemmed from a recurring cocaine habit that first got him suspended in the early 1980s while he was with the Dodgers and resulted in an initial blacklisting in 1986, while he was with the PCL Sacramento Bees. A reprieve materialized when the Texas Rangers secured permission from Commissioner Peter Ueberroth to sign the southpaw for their Oklahoma City farm club, then promoted him to the parent club the following year without the commissioner's approval; while the club was fined $250,000 for its breach of etiquette, it also got to keep the lefthander. Four years after that, Howe was banished a second time, by Commissioner Fay Vincent, following his arrest in Montana for the sale and possession of drugs. This time the Players Association filed a grievance contesting the ban; after pleading *nolo contendere*, Howe was reinstated once again.

Some others whose fates were reconsidered include:

Ray Fisher: Whereas neither the Cleveland Three nor Cobb and Speaker ever missed a game for their perceived transgressions, it took Fisher almost forty years to clear his name. His sin was refusing to sign a one-year contract with the Reds in 1921, choosing instead to end his ten-year career (with a 100–94 record) and become a coach at the University of Michigan. He was blacklisted by Landis without so much as a hearing or even a letter of explanation. Three decades later, the Fisher folder reemerged from the files in the commissioner's office; in it were letters from the Cincinnati club containing a variety of fabrications about the pitcher's refusal to accept a salary increase and his signing with an outlaw club. When it became apparent that Fisher's banishment was the result of nothing more than Cincinnati owner Garry Herrmann's pique at the player for turning down his offer, he was reinstated—more than four decades after the fact. He later worked as a spring-training instructor for the Braves and Tigers.

Rube Benton: When the southpaw accused former Cincinnati manager Buck Herzog of offering him a bribe to throw a 1919 game he was slated to start for the Giants, he set in motion a series of events that included an appearance before the grand jury investigating the Black Sox and a trip to Chicago with NL president John Heydler to find the bartender who supposedly overheard Herzog's offer. When the latter turned into a fiasco, with Benton unable to distinguish among the various saloons-turned-speakeasies they visited, Heydler banned the hurler. A year later, after Benton had enjoyed a successful 1922 season in the minors, Cincinnati owner Garry Herrmann decided that another chance was in order, was rebuffed by Heydler, and appealed to Landis. The commissioner not only reinstated Benton but also took everyone involved in his banishment—Herzog, Heydler, and several sportswriters—to task for their criticism of the pitcher.

Dickie Kerr: The saddest irony of the Black Sox scandal is that Kerr, who was credited with 2 of Chicago's 3 wins in the 1919 World Series, ended up sharing the fate of his teammates who did their best to lose the Series. While sitting out the 1922 season over a $500 difference in Chicago owner Charlie Comiskey's best offer and Kerr's estimate of his worth, the lefthander appeared in a semipro game against some of the blacklisted White Sox players; that was sufficient cause for Commissioner Landis to ban him from the major leagues as well. The punishment was rescinded in time for the 1925 season, but Kerr was never again the same pitcher he had been.

George Steinbrenner: The Yankees' owner voluntarily removed himself from active participation in club affairs in 1990 to escape an imminent suspension by Commissioner Fay Vincent for paying gambler Howard Spira $50,000 to provide damaging information about outfielder Dave Winfield. What was supposed to have been a permanent exile ended in March 1993, when Vincent made Steinbrenner's reinstatement one of his last official acts.

THE OLDEST PLAYERS

These players put off retirement as long as possible.

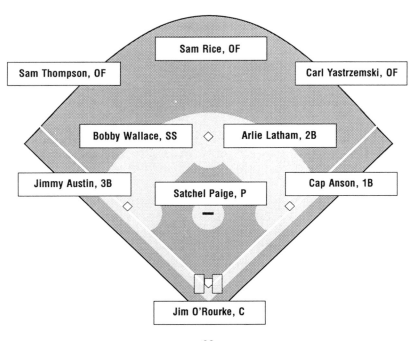

Sam Rice, OF

Sam Thompson, OF

Carl Yastrzemski, OF

Bobby Wallace, SS

Arlie Latham, 2B

Jimmy Austin, 3B

Satchel Paige, P

Cap Anson, 1B

Jim O'Rourke, C

At forty-five, Anson was not only the oldest man ever to play first base; he was also the oldest to play more than 100 games at any position. Since he was also manager of the Cubs in 1897, it might be natural to assume that more than a little ego was involved in his decision to keep himself in the lineup for one more season. But his .285 average in the final season of his twenty-two-year Hall of Fame career goes a long way toward disproving the assumption.

Latham was a year shy of the half-century mark and hadn't played in a big league game in ten years when, while serving as the first full-time coach under Giants' manager John McGraw, he was activated for 4 games, 2 of them at second base, in 1909. The lifetime .269 hitter failed to get a hit in 2 at-bats for New York, but he did become the oldest man ever to steal a base at the big league level.

FRESHEST MAN ON EARTH
NEW YORK GIANTS – COACH   1911

In 1886, Arlie Latham fulfilled a brash eighth-inning prediction that he would tie a postseason championship game by tripling home two runs to send the contest into extra innings.

Austin played one game at the hot corner for the Browns in 1925, 1926, and 1929, the last of them when he was past his forty-ninth birthday; a .246 hitter in eighteen seasons, the switch hitter was 0-for-1 in his final appearance.

Hall of Famer Wallace was forty-four when he appeared in 32 contests—12 of them at short—for the 1918 Cardinals. His .153 average in his final season didn't help his career mark of .266 over twenty-five years.

Thompson, yet another Cooperstown honoree, was forty-six when he added an 8-game footnote to his career in 1906, eight years after he had first retired. His encore, with the Tigers, produced a .226 average, a far cry from his career mark of .331.

Rice played in 97 games (78 of them in the outfield) for the Indians and hit .293 in 1934, his final season. He had spent his first nineteen years with the Senators, for whom he compiled most of the career .322 average that earned him his Cooperstown plaque. He was forty-four when he retired.

Yastrzemski was virtually a full-time designated hitter by the time he turned forty-four in August 1983, but he completes this all–Hall of Fame outfield by having played one of his 119 games that year in the pasture. He hit .266 in the last of his twenty-three years with the Red Sox.

Right up to Carlton Fisk and Bob Boone, over-forty catchers have been more frequent than one might suppose. But Hall of Famer O'Rourke set the standard by becoming the oldest man, at fifty-four, to play all nine innings of a major league game. Following his original retirement, with a .310 average in 1893, he became a successful lawyer and minor league official. In 1904, however, he convinced Giants' manager John McGraw to let him catch a game on September 22, 1904; in what proved to be the pennant-clinching contest, he became the oldest man both to get a base hit and to score a run in a big league contest.

The legendary Paige was an estimated fifty-nine years old when he hurled 3 scoreless innings for the 1965 Athletics. The righthander had been the oldest rookie in history when he debuted with the Indians in 1948, helping the club to a pennant with a 6–1 record and 2.48 ERA. Although the righthander's stint with the Athletics was his last major league performance, Paige was signed by the Atlanta Braves in 1968 so that he could qualify for a pension; he was released, without appearing in a game, as soon as he had logged enough time on the roster, but the ploy made him a major leaguer at sixty-two. Either way, he is the oldest player in history. Paige, too, has a plaque in Cooperstown.

Only Anson among those in this lineup played more than 100 games in the field. Rice joins him by virtue of having appeared in 105 contests in the outfield for the 1931 Senators, when he was forty-one years old. The rest of a team of oldest regulars would be Rabbit Maranville (41, 1933 Braves) at second base; Graig Nettles (42, 1986 Padres) at third; Luke Appling (42, 1949 White Sox) at shortstop; Stan Musial (41, 1962 Cardinals) and Ty Cobb (40, 1927 Athletics) in the outfield; Carlton Fisk (43, 1991 White Sox) behind the plate; and Nolan Ryan (47, 1993 Rangers) on the mound.

Honorable mention to:

Deacon McGuire, a career .278 hitter and a future Hall of Famer who, while a coach for the Tigers in 1912, was prevailed upon to fill in behind the plate during the one-day strike staged by Detroit players in protest over the suspension of Ty Cobb for attacking a spectator; with a bunch of local amateurs as teammates, the forty-six-year-old singled in 2 at-bats, scored a run, and made 3 assists.

Charley O'Leary, who was a few weeks shy of his fifty-second birthday when he convinced Rogers Hornsby, manager of the Browns, to reactivate him from the coaching ranks in 1934. An infielder, mostly with Detroit, between 1904 and 1913, O'Leary claimed he wanted to improve on his .226 lifetime average. Pinch-hitting, he singled, but it wasn't enough to raise his mark to .227.

On August 14, 1932, Jack Quinn became the oldest pitcher ever to win a major league game; the righthander was forty-nine, two years older than Paige's official age when he won his last game. Quinn's victory, for the Dodgers, was the 247th of his twenty-three-year career. Two years earlier, while with the Athletics, he had hit the last of his 8 career home runs; the blast came eight days before his forty-seventh birthday and made him the oldest man ever to clout a four-bagger.

The oldest player to make his major league debut was Diomedes Olivo, who came out of the Pittsburgh bullpen four times in 1960, when he was forty-one years old; he had a 2.79 ERA but no record and no saves. (Paige was slightly younger when he joined Cleveland in 1948.)

The saga of Minnie Minoso stretches over six decades. A popular outfielder with the White Sox, Indians, and two other teams between 1949 and 1964, he returned to the South Side of Chicago to DH and bat .125 in three games in 1976, when he was fifty-three. Four years later, at fifty-seven, he came back yet again to pinch-hit twice, both times unsuccessfully. He would have unretired a third time in 1990, but Commissioner Fay Vincent nixed his attempt to become baseball's only six-decade player.

The pilot of this graybeard crew is Connie Mack, who managed his final game for the Philadelphia Athletics in 1950, when he was a few months shy of his eighty-ninth birthday.

SPECIAL ROSTER SPOTS

Each of the following players held down one of twenty-five spots on various rosters, but not for the usual reasons.

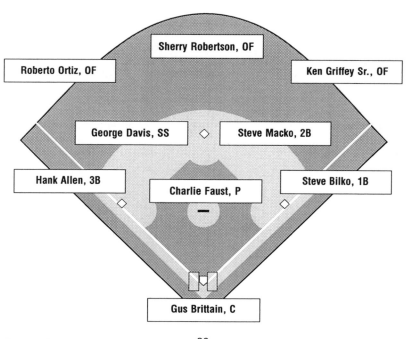

Sherry Robertson, OF

Roberto Ortiz, OF

Ken Griffey Sr., OF

George Davis, SS

Steve Macko, 2B

Hank Allen, 3B

Charlie Faust, P

Steve Bilko, 1B

Gus Brittain, C

Bilko had been such a fan favorite in Los Angeles because of his minor league slugging with the PCL Angels in the the mid-1950s that the Dodgers acquired him from the Reds almost as soon as they arrived in California in 1958. The Angels made equally sure that he was part of their inaugural season in 1961. A bust for the Dodgers (.208 in 47 games), the righty hitter responded to the expansion team's gesture by batting .279 with 20 homers.

Ken Griffey Sr.'s best years came with the Reds in the 1970s and early 1980s.

Even though he was well enough to get into only 6 games, Macko, fatally ill with cancer, was carried on the Cubs' roster throughout the 1980 season as a morale boost for him. He died in November 1981.

Even though Hank Allen, at the end of an undistinguished seven-year career, could manage only 7 hits in 60 at-bats between 1972 and 1973, White Sox manager Chuck Tanner was so enamored of Dick Allen that he made room on the roster for the slugger's older brother in both seasons.

Davis was a victim of the settlement between the AL and NL in 1903. After jumping from the Giants to the White Sox in 1902, he became disillusioned with owner Charlie Comiskey's salary scale and switched back to New York for the 1903 season. After only 4 games with the Polo Grounders, however, he was awarded to Chicago in the peace treaty between the two circuits. Davis refused to report and sat out the rest of the season while he fought a losing court battle over the issue. New York manager John McGraw, never keen on the truce with the AL, kept Davis on his roster all year.

Even though Ortiz, a native Puerto Rican, would appear in only 39 games and hit a mere .202, the Senators kept him around for much of the 1950 season as an interpreter for Cuban pitchers Connie Marrero and Sandy Consuegra. The two righthanders' English must have improved by October, because Ortiz was released before the end of the schedule.

Robertson had no particular skill as either a hitter or fielder, but he was Washington owner Clark Griffith's nephew and heir apparent Calvin Griffith's brother. As a result, he put in ten seasons (between 1940 and 1952) in a Senators uniform, ending up with a .230 batting average.

The arrival of Ken Griffey Jr. on the Mariners in 1989 made the club's purchase of Griffey Sr. from the Reds the following year all but inevitable. The idea, a publicity man's fantasy, was to cash in on the novelty of having a father and son on the same team at the same time, but Griffey *père* turned the move into more than a stunt by hitting .377 in 21 games after he arrived on the West Coast and .282 in 30 games in 1991 before retiring.

Brittain's entire career consisted of one game behind the plate and 2 pinch-hitting appearances for the Reds in 1937. His primary job was to precipitate brawls that manager Chuck Dressen figured would make the last-place team more aggressive. Despite Brittain's best effort in charging out of the dugout to incite several altercations, the Reds still finished last.

The most notable good luck charm in baseball history, Faust tried to convince New York manager John McGraw that the Giants would win the pennant if he were permitted to pitch. While McGraw demurred at the suggestion as long as games meant something in the standings, he did keep Faust around long enough for the club to launch a winning streak. With the players referring to him as Victory, he stuck around for the rest of what was an NL championship season. Faust was recalled during losing streaks in both 1912 and 1913 and claimed a hand in pennants in those years as well. With McGraw's decision that Faust's services were expendable in 1914 coinciding with the mascot's disappearance, the Giants finished 10 1/2 games behind the Miracle Braves. As for Faust, he died in a mental institution the following year. McGraw actually let Faust pitch in 2 games after New York had clinched the pennant in 1911. He gave up a run in 2 innings in what everyone—including the opposition Dodgers but not Faust himself—considered a joke.

Honorable mention to:

Barney Schultz. A bullpen specialist with the Cardinals and two other teams in the late 1950s and 1960s, the knuckleballer was particularly effective in 1964, when his 1.64 ERA and 14 saves helped St. Louis to an NL pennant. Even though his career was over by 1966, the Cardinals kept him on their roster in both 1967 and 1968 so that he could qualify for a pension; several players have been carried on one or another major league roster for one season in order to become vested in the pension fund, but Schultz is the only one thought worthy of the courtesy in two seasons.

All the bonus babies of the 1950s, who were on major league rosters only because of a misguided regulation requiring teams that lavished huge amounts on untested prospects to carry them for two seasons instead of farming them out to the minors. The paradigmatic bonus baby was Tom Qualters of the Phillies, who gave up 6 earned runs in one-third of an inning (a 162.00 ERA) in 1953 and sat in the bullpen for every inning of every game of the 1954 season without once getting a call. He is the last major leaguer to be in uniform for every game of a season without taking part in one. (After two seasons in the minors, the righthander pitched for the Phils and White Sox in 1957 and 1958, but without much success.)

The mid-century St. Louis Browns were so bad that owner Bill DeWitt created the unprecedented position of team hypnotist and hired Dr. David Tracy to fill it. The strategy of artificially inducing self-confidence in the players came a cropper when, shortly after Tracy's arrival in 1950, the Red Sox walloped the Browns by a score of 20–4, following that up by establishing a twentieth-century record for most runs scored in a 29–4 drubbing. The next day, Tracy was sent packing.

LABOR RELATIONS

The history of baseball has been as much about contracts, the reserve clause, and labor strife as hits, runs, and errors. And John Montgomery Ward, Curt Flood, and Andy Messersmith aren't the only players meriting mention in a labor history of baseball.

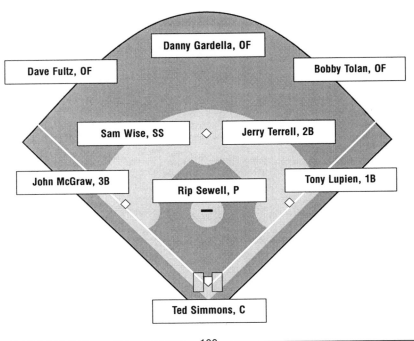

Lupien went to court in 1945 to challenge his demotion to the minor leagues by the Phillies on the grounds that the move violated the right of World War II veterans to reintegration in their jobs. The lifetime .268 hitter settled out of court and eventually worked his way back to the big leagues, with the White Sox, for one more season.

Terrell's religious convictions led him to cast the sole dissenting vote in the Players Association vote to authorize the 1980 spring-training strike. The Kansas City infielder hit only .063 in 1980 and retired after the season with a .253 lifetime mark.

Despite his willingness to sign a contract with the Cardinals in 1900, McGraw made no bones about his intention to jump to the fledgling AL the following season. As a result, he insisted that his contract with St. Louis not include the standard reserve clause; the pact marked the last time until the aftermath of the Messersmith-McNally decision seventy-five years later that a major league team agreed to such a condition.

JOHN McGRAW

John McGraw's tenure in the American League lasted less than two seasons, after which he piloted the Giants until 1932.

Wise was the first player to ignore the reserve clause. After one game with the NL Detroit Wolverines in 1881, the infielder signed a contract for 1882 with Cincinnati of the new AA, then unwisely changed his mind and jumped back to the NL, with Boston. The Reds were denied an injunction preventing Wise from appearing with Boston in what was the first occasion on which major league baseball resorted to the courts to settle its intramural squabbles. For seven seasons Wise remained in Boston, where, on the way to a .272 career average, he became, in 1884, the first player to strike out more than 100 times.

A lifetime .271 hitter in seven seasons as an outfielder around the turn of the century and a lawyer, Fultz organized the Base Ball Players Fraternity in 1912. The organization's relatively minor successes—getting an agreement to provide players with copies of their contracts and written notification when they were released or traded— had less to do with Fultz's skills as a negotiator than with the threat major league owners felt from the formation of the FL in 1914. With the demise of the Feds, Fultz concentrated on improving the lot of minor leaguers and called for a strike toward that end in 1916, initially persuading several hundred major league players to honor the call. The fraternity effectively died when the owners convinced enough of the big leaguers that if they walked out, they would be permanently unemployed.

Of all the players lured to the Mexican League in 1946 by Jorge Pasquel's money, Gardella was the only one to challenge his banishment by Commissioner Happy Chandler. When a federal appeals court supported the former outfielder's position in unequivocal terms, the owners were faced with a choice between proceeding with an appeal to the U.S. Supreme Court or retreating. As a result, Chandler reinstated Gardella and the rest of the jumpers. A few weeks later, Gardella settled out of court. He returned to the major leagues for one at-bat in 1950 and ended his career with a .267 average.

Tolan came as close as anyone else prior to 1975 to undoing the reserve clause. The San Diego outfielder played the entire 1974 season without a contract, then filed two grievances in October. The first, seeking free agency for himself, became moot in December when he agreed to a two-year deal for 1974 and 1975. The other, asking for clarification of ownership's right to renew contracts a year at a time for as long as it saw fit and for as much money as it cared to pay, remained in effect until it was withdrawn by Players Association executive director Marvin Miller on the eve of the Messersmith-McNally decision. Miller made the move both to take the heat off arbitrator Peter Seitz and to encourage the owners to negotiate the terms of the reserve clause.

Simmons was another Messersmith-McNally predecessor who sought to undo free agency when he decided to play the 1972 season for the Cardinals without a contract. The switch hitter stayed unsigned until August 9, when he agreed to a pact covering both 1972 and 1973. He went on to a twenty-one-year career in which he hit .285.

Sewell was the major clubhouse opponent of Robert Murphy's efforts to unionize the Pirates through the American Baseball Guild in 1946. After the initiative failed, Commissioner Happy Chandler gave the righthander a watch for his antilabor stance. Sewell is otherwise remembered as the developer of the crowd-pleasing eephus pitch that reached the plate only after passing through a high arc that tantalized batters.

Honorable mention to:

Catcher Pat Deasley, who persuaded St. Louis owner Chris Von der Ahe to agree to a contract for the 1884 season without a reserve clause. After the season, Deasley solicited offers for the following year from other AA clubs, only to be told that his pact had been a fraud and that the Browns still held the rights to his services.

Pitcher Casey Hageman, whose three-year career and 3–7 record were less memorable than his lawsuit against the Red Sox for sending him to the low minors and slashing his salary in 1913 despite assurances that they would do neither; Fultz's Base Ball Players Fraternity took up his cause and won him a judgment of $2,348, but only after five years of legal wrangling.

First baseman Clarence Kraft, whose demotion from an AA to an A minor league team in 1914 almost precipitated baseball's first general strike; the five hundred or so members of the Players Fraternity were on the verge of walking out when Brooklyn owner Charles Ebbets bought out the claim of the lower-classification team. Later that season, Kraft banged out a single in one of his only 3 major league at-bats, for the Braves.

Pitcher Bob Harris, who suffered the same fate as Lupien after returning from military service in 1946; he, too, settled out of court, but he got only about two-thirds of what he was due and had to endure both the private importunings of a U.S. Attorney to take what was offered and the public pat on his own back by Athletics' owner Connie Mack for his self-proclaimed generosity.

And minor league hurler George Earl Toolson, whose claim that the Yankees had used the reserve clause to keep him from advancing in his profession was rejected by the U.S. Supreme Court in 1953; the High Court upheld its 1922 decision that baseball was exempt from antitrust legislation not on the original grounds that baseball was not commerce but that the remedy for the exemption had to come from Congress.

TEAMMATE TROUBLES

Some teammates play together without liking it very much.

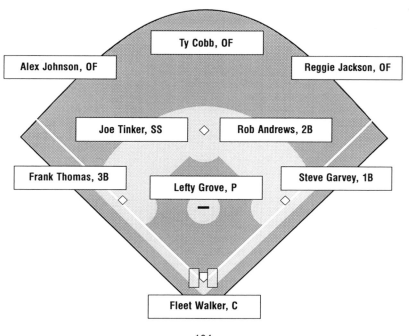

Ty Cobb, OF

Alex Johnson, OF

Reggie Jackson, OF

Joe Tinker, SS

Rob Andrews, 2B

Frank Thomas, 3B

Steve Garvey, 1B

Lefty Grove, P

Fleet Walker, C

Garvey's Mr. Clean image, Dodger-blue bleeding, obvious affection for every camera he saw, and unabashed political aspirations were so cloying to Los Angeles teammates in the 1970s that they led to several clubhouse scuffles, most notably with pitcher Don Sutton.

Andrews was a central figure in the born-again Christian God Squad of the Giants in the late 1970s that, in the view of critics, equated success on the diamond, or lack of it, to the designs of a higher power. This led to charges of lack of aggressiveness, divided the San Francisco clubhouse into warring factions, and caused the firing of two managers. Andrews hit .251 in his five major league seasons.

Not even Thomas's ninth-inning, pinch-hit, game-tying home run for the Phillies on July 3, 1965, could save him from being released after the contest because of a violent fight with Dick Allen earlier in the day, during batting practice, over perceived racial attitudes. Thomas caught on with the Astros but ended his career the following year with a .266 average and 286 homers.

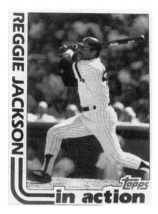

Reggie Jackson, the straw that stirred the Yankees' drink in the late 1970s.

Tinker got miffed at keystone partner Johnny Evers over a mix-up concerning a taxi and, the linkage of their names in baseball lore notwithstanding, refused to speak to the second baseman for thirty-three years.

Cobb's defensiveness about being a southern Protestant on a Detroit team filled with Irish- and German-Catholic northerners led to so many conflicts with fellow outfielders Marty McIntyre, Sam Crawford, and Davy Jones that manager Hughie Jennings took to shifting their positions day to day so that only the one feeling least homicidal toward Cobb on any given afternoon would have to play next to him. For his part, Cobb took to carrying a pistol after a hotel lobby fistfight with pitcher Ed Siever in 1906. It fell to catcher—and ex-prizefighter—Boss Schmidt to serve as team enforcer and whip the outfielder whenever he became more obstreperous than usual.

Johnson's mental instability while he was with the Angels in the early 1970s resulted in run-ins that had several teammates going after him—most notably, Ken

Berry with his fists, and the equally unstable Chico Ruiz, with a gun. After the Ruiz incident, the Angels suspended Johnson, but the outfielder won a grievance that required the club to put him on the disabled list for his emotional problems.

Jackson, the self-proclaimed "straw that stirs the drink," was especially successful in stirring up Graig Nettles and Thurman Munson when he arrived at Yankee Stadium in 1977.

The first black player in the major leagues, Walker had particular trouble with batterymate Tony Mullane on the AA Toledo Blue Stockings in 1884. When it became apparent that if the hurler wasn't deliberately bouncing balls in front of the plate, he was ignoring every sign in an effort to embarrass the receiver, the two reached an unspoken pact to dispense with signals altogether. Without recanting the racist attitude behind his behavior, Mullane later praised Walker as "the best catcher I ever worked with" for his ability to handle pitches without knowing what was coming.

Grove's notorious temper sent substitute outfielder Jimmy Moore running for cover after making an error in a 1931 game that cost the southpaw his seventeenth consecutive win. From his hiding place, Moore could hear Grove tearing apart the clubhouse while damning the culprit who had cost him a new AL record. The outfielder's terror abated only when he realized that the object of Grove's wrath was regular Athletics' left fielder Al Simmons, on whose absence Grove blamed the miscue.

Special mention to:

Rube Waddell of the 1908 Athletics. Manager Connie Mack had always pampered the Hall of Fame lefthander despite his erratic habits, and Waddell had responded with four 20-win seasons. But an injury prior to the 1905 World Series diminished the southpaw's effectiveness and impelled his eccentricity toward a sometimes violent instability. One glaring example was a tantrum he threw after blowing a 7–1 lead against the Tigers in late September 1907. Several teammates became so fed up with the southpaw's antics that they let Mack know that they would not report to training camp the following spring if Waddell was still on the roster. The manager shipped his erstwhile ace to the Browns after the 1907 season.

Ray Schalk of the 1919 White Sox. No one had better reason to detest his teammates than the receiver who watched as several of them threw the World Series to the Reds. So furious was he with what was happening that he shoved umpire Cy Rigler in a dispute over a close play at the plate in the sixth inning of Game 5 and got thrown out of the contest. But the catcher's animus was less toward the arbiter than toward center fielder Happy Felsch for dropping an easy fly ball and pitcher Lefty Williams for ignoring his signals. The catcher later worked Williams over with his fists for his complicity in the Black Sox' perfidy.

Babe Ruth and Lou Gehrig. The causes of the feud between the two greatest hitters in Yankee history are obscure. Nearing the end of his career in the early 1930s, Ruth picked fights at the slightest provocation. He and his wife apparently took offense at some disparaging remarks by Gehrig's mother about their child-rearing abilities. One comment led to another, and Gehrig, once Ruth's friend and admirer, broke off the relationship. The pair did not speak again until Lou Gehrig Day in 1939, after the first baseman had been diagnosed with amyotrophic lateral sclerosis, when Ruth, attending the reunion of the 1927 team in Gehrig's honor, gave him a public bear hug, a scene reenacted in the Hollywood film *The Pride of the Yankees*.

Billy North of the 1974 A's. In the most notorious clubhouse incident involving the brawling Oakland clubs of the early 1970s, North squared off against Reggie Jackson. Catcher Ray Fosse intervened and suffered a crushed disk in his neck that forced him to miss the rest of the season.

MANAGER TROUBLES

Members of this team would have preferred someone else calling the shots.

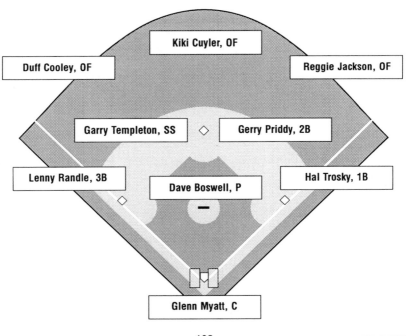

Kiki Cuyler, OF

Duff Cooley, OF

Reggie Jackson, OF

Garry Templeton, SS

Gerry Priddy, 2B

Lenny Randle, 3B

Dave Boswell, P

Hal Trosky, 1B

Glenn Myatt, C

Trosky was a leader of the so-called Cry Baby Indians who revolted in 1940 against manager Ossie Vitt's public mocking and disparaging of his players. Trosky and his compatriots virtually ignored the pilot's signs and established their own set of signals to countermand instructions from the bench. They were also known to start fights in the hope that Vitt would get involved. The manager was fired at the end of the season. Trosky hit .302 and drove in more than 100 runs in six of his eleven seasons with the Indians and White Sox.

Priddy became an unwanted presence by loudly declining to join other members of the 1947 Senators in signing a letter drawn up by manager Ossie Bluege expressing the team's admiration for its skipper. Priddy refused to shrink from the general perception that Bluege was mismanaging the pitching staff and lacked the guts to protest to owner Clark Griffth about travel arrangements that on more than one occasion had left the team stranded without hotel rooms. At the end of the season, the second baseman was traded to the Browns.

Kiki Cuyler teamed with Hack Wilson and Riggs Stephenson on the Cubs to form what was arguably the best outfield of the twentieth century.

Randle assaulted manager Frank Lucchesi at the Rangers' spring-training camp in 1977, delivering a sucker punch while the pilot was talking to reporters and pummeling the skipper even after he fell to the ground. His only excuse was that he was tired of being called a punk by Lucchesi, who denied the charge from his hospital bed. Randle was suspended, fined, arrested, and eventually traded to the Mets.

In 1981, Templeton gave the finger to Busch Stadium fans for tormenting him over what they regarded as his overly casual performance. St. Louis manager Whitey Herzog responded by pulling him down the dugout steps and shoving him onto the bench, then making sure he was traded after the season—to San Diego for Ozzie Smith—despite a hospital stay for depression. The switch hitter is otherwise remembered as the first player to get 100 hits from each side of the plate in a single season.

Cooley was the ringleader and spokesman for a contingent of Phillies who demanded the ouster of manager George Stallings almost immediately after he was appointed in 1897. The causes of the rebellion were the pilot's affinity for harsh regulations and profane tongue lashings. Stallings was fired in the middle of the 1898 season; Cooley spent thirteen seasons in the big leagues, batting .294.

Cuyler protested when Pittsburgh manager Donie Bush moved him from third to second in the batting order to help shake a team slump in 1927. Cuyler asserted that he was better at driving in runs than at the hit-and-run, and to underline the point, he went hitless from his new spot in a few games. One shouting match led to another, and Cuyler found himself on the bench, replaced by Clyde Barnhart for the rest of the season and the World Series against the Yankees and then traded to the Cubs for infielder Sparky Adams and outfielder Pete Scott, whose careers included nothing as memorable as Cuyler's .321 average and Hall of Fame plaque.

Jackson's arrival on the Yankees in 1977 didn't make manager Billy Martin any happier than it made catcher Thurman Munson. For his part, the lefty slugger spent a good deal of time sulking about Martin's decisions to drop him from the cleanup spot or relegate him to being a DH. The tableau that defines their relationship is the scene that ensued after Martin had replaced Jackson in right field in mid-inning after he played a routine bloop single into a double: National television cameras caught the outfielder screaming at his manager, with the latter trying to break away from several coaches who were restraining him from attacking the player.

Myatt was let go by the Indians in the middle of 1935 because of assertions by manager Walter Johnson that the veteran catcher and third baseman Willie Kamm were the ringleaders of a plot to get rid of him. However, when club president Billy Evans publicly applauded the decision of the Giants to sign the thirty-eight-year-old Myatt, it became apparent that Johnson's days in Cleveland were numbered as well. In fact, he failed to finish the season.

The details surrounding Boswell's epic thrashing by Minnesota manager Billy Martin in 1969 are murky at best, but the most commonly repeated version is that the pilot intervened in a barroom fight between the righthander and outfielder Bob Allison, took a shot not intended for him, and proceeded to work the pitcher over while two other patrons held him. Martin came out on top, at least temporarily: Boswell was fined for starting the brawl, and the team finished at the top of the AL West; but when the Twins were swept by the Orioles in the League Championship Series (LCS), club owner Calvin Griffith found the excuse he had been looking for to fire Martin.

Other memorable pilot-player encounters include:

Babe Ruth and Miller Huggins of the Yankees in 1923: Even while recuperating from the celebrated spring-training bellyache that kept him out of the lineup until June, the Bambino continued to ignore the manager's curfews and field tactics. In late August, Huggins slapped his star slugger with a $5,000 fine and an indefinite suspension for showing up late for a game one too many times. Ruth issued a him-or-me ultimatum and set out for owner Jake Ruppert's office, but instead of the vindication he anticipated, the Babe had to listen to Ruppert's assertion to reporters that "Huggins is in complete command" and apologize publicly to his teammates.

Phil Linz and Yogi Berra of the Yankees in 1964: Linz started playing his infamous harmonica solo on the team bus after a fourth straight loss by the New Yorkers. When Berra suggested that the musician shove his instrument, the utility infielder tossed both the mouth organ and a suggestion that he try at the manager. The incident convinced club president Del Webb and general manager Ralph Houk that Berra had lost control of the club and that he would have to go after the season whether or not he won a pennant. He did finish first, and he was fired.

The Giants and Alvin Dark in 1964: While Berra was objecting to Linz's musical inclinations, Dark was disparaging the black and Latin players on his team for their lack of mental alertness and pride. The impetus toward baseball's first racial strike was halted only by the intervention of Willie Mays, who pointed out that however repulsive the manager's racial views were, they never stopped him from fielding a majority of blacks and Hispanics. Mays's intercession enabled Dark to hold on to his job, but only for the rest of the season.

FRONT OFFICE TROUBLES

These players were either ruffled—or felt ruffled by—team owners or general managers.

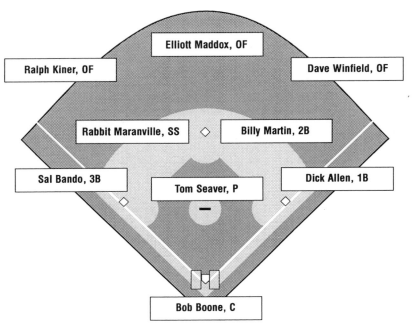

Elliott Maddox, OF

Ralph Kiner, OF

Dave Winfield, OF

Rabbit Maranville, SS

Billy Martin, 2B

Sal Bando, 3B

Tom Seaver, P

Dick Allen, 1B

Bob Boone, C

Declaring the White Sox a second-class operation, Allen quit the team sixteen days before the end of the 1974 season (and still won the AL home-run title). The slugger had a change of heart in the offseason, but owner Arthur Allyn and general manager Rollie Hemond didn't and shipped the slugger to Atlanta for $5,000 and a second-string catcher.

A brawl at the Copacabana in the middle of the 1957 season was all the excuse Yankee general manager George Weiss needed to ship Martin to Kansas City. Already convinced that Martin was a bad influence on Mickey Mantle and Whitey Ford, Weiss chose to ignore that it was actually outfielder Hank Bauer who slugged the victim, that the fight took place in a men's room while Martin was in the nightclub proper, and that the whole affair was a response to racist heckling of performer Sammy Davis Jr.

Bando declared that his decision to end years of animosity with owner Charlie Finley and leave Oakland for free agency after the 1976 season was "like leaving the *Titanic* before it went down."

Ralph Kiner had a higher ratio of home runs to at-bats than any other player except Babe Ruth.

Cubs' president Bill Veeck Sr. thought he had found a solution to dealing with perennial cutup Maranville by naming him player-manager of the team in 1925. The experiment lasted only a few weeks, during which the infielder took his players out to celebrate every win as if it were a World Series victory, engaged in a headline-making fight with a Brooklyn cabdriver, emptied a spittoon on fellow train passengers, and made life generally hell for traveling secretary John Seys.

Kiner's war with Pittsburgh president Branch Rickey ended in June 1953 with the latter's announcement that "we can finish last without you" and the outfielder's departure to the Cubs. Ever since the executive's arrival in Pittsburgh in 1950, he had been irritated by Kiner's visibility in everything from labor causes to Hollywood gossip columns and by the popularity of his one-dimensional slugging skills. Kiner, in turn, was disgusted with what he saw as his boss's parsimonious and dishonest approach to contract negotiations.

Maddox became an embarrassment to the Mets when he pursued a lawsuit against

Shea Stadium for an injury suffered while he was with the Yankees during their exile in Queens. He was released at the end of the 1980 season and never played another major league game.

Winfield's ongoing strife with Yankees' owner George Steinbrenner surfaced in 1990 when an investigation by Commissioner Fay Vincent's office revealed that Steinbrenner had paid professional gambler Howard Spira $40,000 for information damaging to Winfield. The dispute centered on Spira's onetime employer, the Winfield Foundation, a charitable trust designed to fund youth programs and supported by direct payments from the Yankees as part of the outfielder's $23-million, ten-year contract; it worsened when the Boss refused to provide the called-for cash until what he perceived as financial irregularities had been straightened out. When the dust settled, Winfield had departed for the Angels via free agency, and Steinbrenner had agreed to remove himself from club affairs permanently rather than have the commissioner formally suspend him for associating with known gamblers.

Boone was sold to the Angels in retaliation for his role as NL player representative in the 1981 strike. Phillies' owner Robert Carpenter was so upset by the labor action that he sold not only the catcher but also, within the year, the franchise, too.

Seaver's public feud with Mets' chairman M. Donald Grant began in 1977, when the pitcher expressed doubts about the organization's commitment to winning absent a willingness to sign frontline free agents. It reached critical mass when *New York Daily News* columnist Dick Young suggested that the righthander's criticism of the front office had more than a little to do with his wife's envy that Nolan Ryan was getting more money from the Angels. It ended with the hurler's trade to the Reds on June 15. The aftermath of what came to be called the Midnight Massacre included a tearful televised departure by the player known as the Franchise, canceled season tickets, a picket line of fans, and enough menacing calls to Grant's office for the chairman to hire a bodyguard for the rest of the year.

Some other notable encounters between executives and performers:

Charley Jones and Arthur Soden of the 1880 Braves: The archetype of the skinflint owner, Soden often delayed paychecks. On one such occasion, slugging outfielder Jones complained that he hadn't seen a check in three weeks. The owner responded that they would discuss the matter when the team returned to Boston from a road trip, then stranded the player in Cleveland and accused him of jumping the team. Jones remained blackballed from the game for all of 1881 and 1882.

The 1947 Yankees and Larry MacPhail: On the edge of a nervous breakdown all season, club president MacPhail drove everyone to distraction with his manic devotion to promotional events, even going so far as to fine Joe DiMaggio for failure to attend one. Equally enamored of air travel, he forced the club to travel around the league in an old C-54 military transport that narrowly avoided accidents on several occasions. Only the intervention of DiMaggio and manager Bucky Harris headed off a player insurrection. Team physician Mal Stevens, on the other hand, resigned in disgust over the owner's incessant interference even in his department. MacPhail sold his share of the team after the World Series.

Johnny Lindell and George Weiss of the Yankees in the late 1940s: Weiss's phobia about the carousing of his charges led him to hire ubiquitous detectives to catch the culprits. Among the most flagrant in flaunting the rules was outfielder Lindell, who took great satisfaction in the investigators' fees Weiss spent pursuing him. Even manager Bucky Harris got into the act. Ordered by Weiss to read some of the more revealing details in the reports at a clubhouse meeting, the pilot complied, but in a tone that left little doubt where his sympathies in the matter lay.

The Angels and Dick Walsh, 1969–71: Dubbed the Smiling Python by his less than admiring players, Walsh became so unpopular with members of the Angels that trying to hit him with line drives during batting practice became one of their chief diversions. Among the general manager's less appealing indiscretions was sending a letter to the home of one pitcher advising him that he would receive no raise for the following year because he had contracted a venereal disease; when the hurler's wife opened the letter, she set out for the nearest divorce lawyer.

SCREWBALLS

Somewhere between, on the one hand, the studied pregame antics of official clowns, from Al Schacht and Max Patkin to the San Diego Chicken and the Philly Phanatic, and, on the other hand, the alcohol- or drug-induced escapades of a host of Hall of Famers and lesser lights, there has always been room in baseball for the authentically zany.

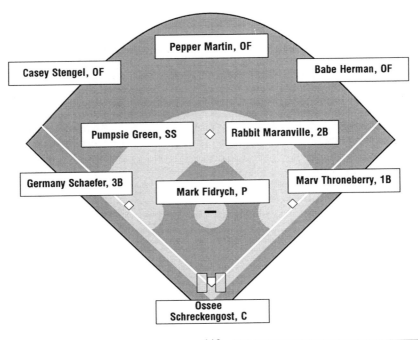

Throneberry became the darling of the New Breed fans of the expansion Mets in the early 1960s for his less than adept fielding and baserunning. The first baseman earned the nickname Marvelous Marv from club owner Joan Payson for hitting a game-winning home run, but it stuck, with an altered emphasis, for such antics as legging out a triple, only to be called out for having neglected to tag second base; when manager Casey Stengel set out to protest the call, the umpires told him not to bother, for the hitter had also failed to touch first.

Maranville was the classic cutup both before and after he stopped drinking in 1927, well into his twenty-three-year Hall of Fame career. The inventor of the basket catch later associated with Willie Mays, Maranville's other on-field antics included putting a pair of glasses on an umpire during an argument, entering the batter's box through the legs of a home-plate umpire, and painting iodine all over the face of still a third arbiter on the pretext of ministering to a scratch. Away from the diamond, the shortstop walked

BABE HERMAN
CATCH A "BASEBALL" FROM A PLANE

Whatever his deficiencies in the field or on the bases, Babe Herman hit .324 in 13 seasons, with a high of .393 in 1930.

on the ledges of hotels, dangled teammates from windows, and created general havoc on trains between cities. For all practical purposes, his career ended when he broke several bones sliding into home in a spring-training game in 1934; so intense was the pain from his injuries that he begged on-deck batter Shanty Hogan to knock him out. The catcher obliged with a single punch.

Schaefer earned his niche in baseball lore by stealing first base. Most accounts place the play in 1908, while the second baseman was with the Tigers, and have him executing the back end of a double steal without drawing a throw from a Cleveland catcher. Safe at second, he reversed direction and went back to first on the next pitch. When this unique ploy also failed to produce the desired throw, he stole second again, and the runner on third finally scored either because the pitcher held the ball too long or the catcher finally got the point and tried to nab Schaefer. His cleverness is often cited as the direct cause of a new rule prohibiting running the bases in reverse, but, in fact, the regulation was not amended until 1920.

Best known as the first black player on the Red Sox, the last team to integrate (in 1959), Green also earned a reputation for flakiness when he and pitcher Gene Conley, distressed over a loss to the Yankees and a Manhattan traffic jam, left the team bus and caught a cab to the airport with a notion to fly to Israel. Lacking passports, they had to settle for wandering around New York before catching up with the team in Washington a few days later.

Long before he became the "Ole Perfessor" or a venerable wiseacre, Stengel was a brash, young clown who baited umpires by carrying a flashlight onto the field to prove his contention that it was too dark to continue a game and by coaching at third base with an open umbrella to demonstrate the futility of continuing another contest in what he considered a downpour. Stengel's most famous stunt as a player was tipping his hat to the crowd and freeing a bird.

Herman may never have been hit on the head by a fly ball (although he was fond of declaring that the shoulder didn't count), and he certainly never tripled into a triple play (as legend has it), but he did double into a double play and enjoyed playing up his reputation as a defensive oaf. Perhaps his greatest moment as a crowd pleaser was his return to a Brooklyn uniform in 1945, after eight years of retirement, when he singled in his first at-bat—and then tripped over first base.

Martin was at the center of the rowdy Gas House Gang Cardinals of the 1930s. Noted for his flashy baserunning on the field, he spent the rest of his time playing in a mudcat band he formed, catching snakes for the St. Louis Zoo, riding fire engines, and driving midget racing cars—all to the detriment of the peace of mind of manager Frankie Frisch and general manager Branch Rickey. Perhaps his most dangerous act of derring-do was a refusal ever to wear an athletic supporter on the field.

Schreckengost was the (relatively) sober half, along with lefthander Rube Waddell, of the Philadelphia battery that blew away AL hitters in the early years of the century and drove A's manager Connie Mack to distraction with their hijinks. Mack later compared Schreckengost to the best catchers in the history of the game for his ability to handle pitchers and to Harpo Marx for his antic spirit.

The rookie Fidrych fascinated Detroit teammates, opponents, and fans in 1972 by talking to the ball, grooming the mound on his hands and knees, and shaking the hand of every infielder who made a good play. His ingenuousness attracted huge crowds around the circuit until injuries curtailed his career prematurely.

Other baseball eccentrics included:

Brickyard Kennedy was the model small-town boy at a loss to deal with the big city. A four-time 20-game winner for the Dodgers at the end of the last century, the righthander never quite got the hang of maneuvering his way around Brooklyn and New York City. In his most legendary escapade, he set out one morning from his Brooklyn home for a game at the Polo Grounds, got lost, and ended up on a train headed for the Midwest. Asked how he could possibly have made such an unlikely mistake, Kennedy shrugged and said that a policeman he had asked for directions "heard I was from Ohio and figured that was where I should be."

Jimmy St. Vrain, a southpaw hurler with the 1902 Cubs, customarily batted from the right side but rarely made contact. Heeding the advice of manager Frank Selee to try hitting lefthanded, he moved to the other side of the plate in a game against the Pirates; from this unfamiliar vantage point, he grounded to shortstop Honus Wagner and was so astonished at his success that he ran as fast as he could—to third base.

Johnny Dickshot of the 1937 Pirates earned his niche in baseball lore by allowing 2 runs to score one windy afternoon when his cap blew off and he elected to chase it rather than a line drive in the gap.

As both a player (in the 1940s) and manager (in the 1950s and 1960s), Bobby Bragan regularly ignored baseball decorum. On one occasion, he argued with an umpire while reclining on his side, elbow to the ground and head in his hand; on another, he responded to being ejected from a game by returning to the field with a soft drink and a straw and offering each of the umpires a sip. Also, Bragan allegedly placed a hex on the Indians for firing him in 1958. The spell has been credited with keeping the team an also-ran for decades; it was lifted, amid much promotional fanfare, by a witch in 1986.

THE NAME OF THE GAME

We would love to tell you that there was once a major leaguer named Barney Baseball. But we can't. Nor has there ever been one named Nestor Nohit or Harry Homerun. Until there is, we will go with:

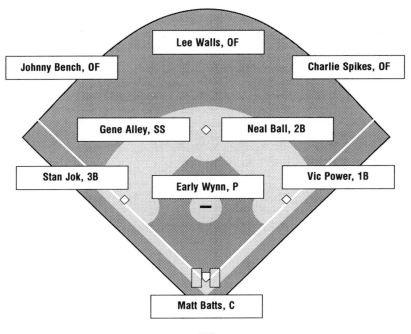

Power's power was only average (126 home runs in twelve seasons), but he did carry a .284 average and the flashiest first baseman's glove of his time around with him to seven teams, from 1954 to 1965.

An otherwise obscure seven-year middle infielder, Ball is best remembered for one play while a member of the 1910 Indians, when he caught a ball off the bat of Boston's Amby McConnell to start the first unassisted triple play in the twentieth century.

Jok hung his up after only two seasons (1954 and 1955 with the Phillies and White Sox) in which he hit only .158.

Alley hit more than a few there (stroking more than 20 doubles and reaching double figures in triples once) in his eleven seasons in the 1960s and 1970s with the Pirates.

Walls, on the other hand, had only one season in which he cleared them with any frequency. In 1958, while with the Cubs, he clouted 24 of his (decade-long) career 66 homers.

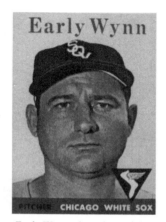

Early Wynn often claimed that his grandmother was the only one he wouldn't brush back— unless she was crowding the plate.

Hall of Famer Bench was too good a hitter to ride one; that's why he sometimes played the outfield when he took a day off from his catching duties.

Spikes took his off for the last time in 1980, after a nine-year career in which he hit .246 for four teams.

Batts didn't do much with his (a .269 average and only 26 homers) in a journeyman career from 1947 to 1956.

Wynn finally got his 300th in 1963, after twenty-three seasons with the Senators, Indians, and White Sox.

Bob Walk could stroll in from the bullpen, but his name hardly inspires a great deal of confidence.

Cecil Fielder could come in for defensive purposes.

And, of course, Herb Score would be up in the announcers' booth doing the play-by-play.

COLORS

This is unquestionably the most colorful team possible.

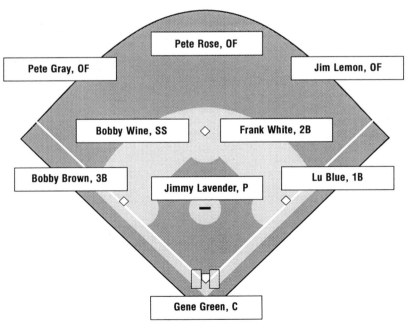

Blue's lifetime .287 average with the Tigers and three other teams from 1921 to 1933 was nothing to be sad about.

White, a .255 hitter, shares (with Ed Kranepool of the Mets) a spotless record for spending the most seasons (eighteen), among non–Hall of Famers, with one club.

Brown's questionable defense muddied the perception of his offensive accomplishments, a .279 average in eight years (1946–54) with the Yankees; he also hit .439 in four World Series. The lefty swinger later became a noted cardiologist and, still later, president of the AL.

Wine's batting average (.215 in twelve seasons between 1960 and 1972, for the Phillies and Expos) wasn't very robust, but he was a slick fielder who, for almost a decade, held the record for most double plays in a season.

His own surliness and the publicity Gray received as a one-armed outfielder for the Browns in 1945 cast a cloud over his relations with his teammates; he hit a powerless .218 and returned to the minors in 1946.

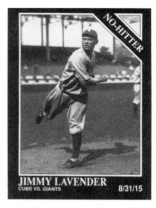

JIMMY LAVENDER
CUBS VS. GIANTS   8/31/15

Spitballer Jimmy Lavender was the pitcher who ended Rube Marquard's 19-game winning streak in 1913.

The all-time leader in hits (4,256 for the Reds, Phillies, and Expos from 1963 to 1986), Rose's prospects for gaining admission to the Hall of Fame are less than rosy because of his indefinite suspension for gambling.

Despite the frequency with which he struck out (three AL-leading totals), Lemon wasn't a lemon; he hit more than 30 homers and drove home 100 runs for the lowly Senators in 1959 and 1960. In twelve seasons (between 1950 and 1963) he hit .262 for Washington and four other teams.

Green's .267 average didn't make anyone envious because he spent more time on the bench than he did on the field during his seven seasons (1957–63) with five teams.

Lavender had no reason to blush after a six-year (1912–17) big league career in which he won in double figures five times but lost in double figures an equal number of times for the Cubs; his greatest claim to fame is that he was the winning pitcher in the game that ended Rube Marquard's 19-game winning streak.

FOOD

Not a very delicious ensemble:

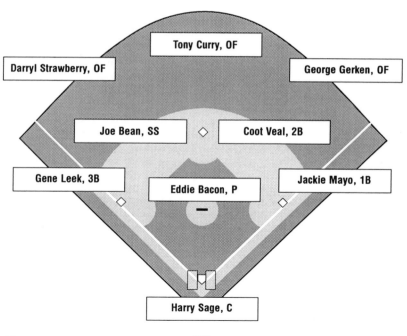

Tony Curry, OF

Darryl Strawberry, OF

George Gerken, OF

Joe Bean, SS

Coot Veal, 2B

Gene Leek, 3B

Eddie Bacon, P

Jackie Mayo, 1B

Harry Sage, C

Mayo spread himself pretty thin as a backup out-fielder and once-in-a-while first baseman for the Phillies in the late 1940s and early 1950s; he hit only .213 and never appeared in more than 50 games in any season.

Veal compiled a not very juicy .231 average as a backup shortstop and occasional second baseman for the Tigers, Senators, and Pirates in a six-season career (1958–1963).

Like an onion, Leek could manage only a .221 average for the Indians and Angels in 1959, 1961, and 1962.

Bean came up with the Giants as a green rookie in 1902. He managed to get into a mere 48 games, in which he hit .222, and never came back.

Some people think dessert is the best part of a meal, and on this team they would be right. Straw-berry has a .259 average and 297 homers after thirteen major league seasons (through 1995) with the Mets, Dodgers, Giants, and Yankees.

Darryl Strawberry's single season with the Yankees in 1995 produced more hype than playing time.

Curry's .246 average in 129 games for the Phillies and Indians in the 1960s wasn't very hot.

Gerken's .225 for Cleveland in only 44 contests in 1927 and 1928 was downright sour.

Sage's .149 average added little spice to the AA Toledo franchise in 1890.

Bacon didn't exactly sizzle when he gave up 4 earned runs on 5 hits and 7 walks in the 6 innings he pitched for the Athletics in 1917.

If he doesn't sour on the assignment, Bob Lemon could be the manager.

At least the pitching staff is a particularly well balanced collection: Herb Hash as a main course; Laurin Pepper, Hap Collard, and Harry Colliflower as vegetables; and Frank Pears, Earl Huckleberry, and Mark Lemongello for dessert.

And what about Johnny Grubb as a pinch hitter?

FISH

Quite a catch:

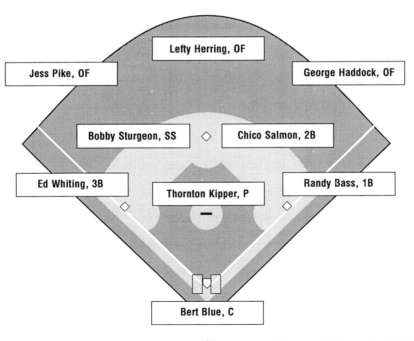

Bass was all at sea in his six seasons (1977–82) with the Twins, Royals, Expos, Padres, and Rangers; he hit only .212 in 130 games.

Salmon was swimming upstream for most of his nine-year career, batting .249 while playing all over the infield and outfield for the Indians and Orioles from 1964 to 1972.

Whiting was a croaker with his .255 for Baltimore and Louisville in the AA and Washington in the NL over four seasons, between 1882 and 1886.

There was no caviar in Sturgeon's six seasons (in the 1940s) with the Cubs and Braves; he managed only a .257 average.

Pike lasted only 16 games with the 1946 Giants, who threw him back to the minors because his .171 average was too small.

Herring might as well have been pickled after two seasons (1899 and 1904) in which he hit a mere .191 with Washington clubs in both the NL and AL.

No one coddled Haddock for his .227 average for six teams between 1888 and 1894.

PADRES
RANDY BASS

Whatever success Randy Bass had as a big leaguer came for the Padres in 1980, when he homered in his first at-bat in a San Diego uniform and hit .286 in 19 games.

Even though Blue's .273 average is the highest for the players on this team, he couldn't have made much of a splash, since he only lasted 17 games, with the Browns and Athletics in 1908.

Kipper's 3–4 record and 5.27 ERA for the Phillies from 1953 to 1955 is preserved forever in the record book.

The Trout family (Dizzy and Steve), Clarence Pickrel, and Preacher Roe round out the pitching staff.

Honorable mention to all the past and present Marlins of Florida and future Devil Rays of Tampa Bay.

ANIMALS

Some ferocious, some tame, even a rodent.

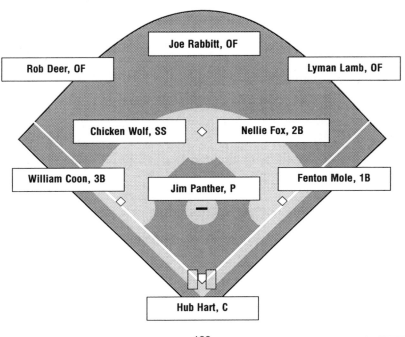

Joe Rabbitt, OF

Rob Deer, OF

Lyman Lamb, OF

Chicken Wolf, SS

Nellie Fox, 2B

William Coon, 3B

Fenton Mole, 1B

Jim Panther, P

Hub Hart, C

Mole was in the dark for most of his 10-game career with the 1949 Yankees; he hit only .185.

Fox was perhaps the best second baseman of his time (1947–65) and one of the cleverest batters of any era; he compiled a .288 average for the Athletics, White Sox, and Astros.

Coon hit .227 for the Philadelphia Athletics in the NL's inaugural season of 1876; after that he was up a tree.

Wolf voraciously attacked AA pitching at a .290 career clip; he is the only one to have played in all ten of the AA's seasons (1882–91) and added a final year in the NL.

Deer hit .220 with 226 homers. But he couldn't run any more than he could cut down on his swing; his stolen base total in ten seasons (1984–93) with four clubs was only 43, and he struck out more often (1,379 times) than he got a base hit (844 of them). His ratio of whiffs to safeties is the worst in major league history.

Rob Deer's 186 strikeouts for the Brewers in 1987 are an American League record.

Rabbitt hopped out of the major leagues after only two games with the 1922 Indians despite a .333 average.

Lamb didn't always go quietly; in two years with the Browns (1920–21) he batted .272.

As a backup catcher for the White Sox from 1905 to 1907, Hart was only swift enough to steal one base to go along with his .218 average.

Panther's 7–13 record and 5.22 ERA weren't very sleek; he pitched for Oakland, Texas, and Atlanta from 1971 to 1973.

Panther is joined in the starting rotation by Lerton Pinto, Bob Moose, Al Doe, and Joe Gibbon.

Honorable mention to all the Tigers of Detroit, Cubs of Chicago, and future Diamondbacks of Arizona.

COUNTRIES

The only thing more comprehensive than an All-Star team is an all–United Nations team. For example:

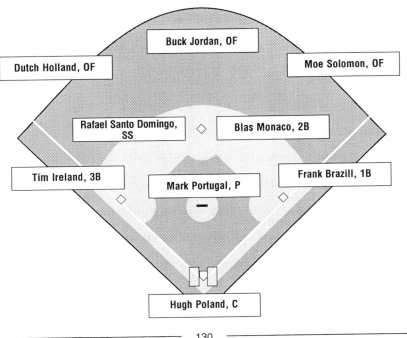

Brazill's .258 average for the 1921–22 Athletics didn't send anyone out to dance in the streets.

The Indians gambled on Monaco twice, once in 1937 and again in 1946, even though he could manage only a .154 average in a total of 17 games.

Ireland couldn't hit for potatoes; his average in 11 games for the Royals in 1981 and 1982 was only .143

Santo Domingo, who was born in Puerto Rico, played in 7 games for the 1979 Reds and managed only a .167 batting average.

Holland hit .273 in 102 games for the Braves (1932–33) and Indians (1934), but he might as well have been wearing wooden shoes, since he stole only one base and didn't cover much territory in the outfield.

Jordan's hitting was no desert; he averaged .299, mostly as a first baseman, for the Braves and four other teams over ten seasons, between 1927 and 1938.

Solomon was born not on a Pacific island but on Manhattan Island. The lefthanded hitter was one of the periodic attempts by Giants' manager John McGraw to find a Jewish player who would appeal to New York's large Jewish population. In an effort to offset some of the popularity of the Yankees' Babe Ruth, McGraw heralded Solomon as the Rabbi of Swat. Despite 3 hits (none of them home runs) in 8 at-bats for the Giants in 1923, the outfielder was such a major defensive liability that he was gone after only 2 games.

No joke, Poland hit .185 as a backup catcher in 83 games for four NL clubs in the 1940s.

Even though it is unlikely to inspire a sonnet, Portugal's 84-67 record (and 3.79 ERA) with the Twins, Astros, Giants, and Reds over the past eleven seasons is more than respectable.

And in the bullpen Ossie France and Hector Trinidad take turns throwing to Gus Brittain.

Mark Portugal's best season came for Houston in 1993, when he led National League hurlers with an .818 won-lost percentage for his 18–4 record.

THE GOD SQUAD

If prayer helps, this team might never lose a game.

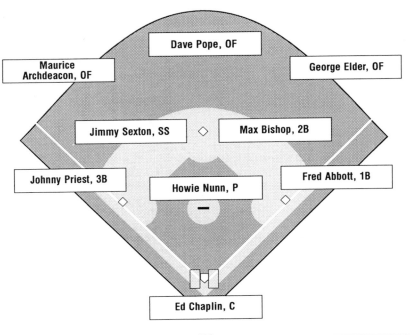

Dave Pope, OF

Maurice Archdeacon, OF

George Elder, OF

Jimmy Sexton, SS

Max Bishop, 2B

Johnny Priest, 3B

Howie Nunn, P

Fred Abbott, 1B

Ed Chaplin, C

It was vespers for Abbott after he put together only a .209 average as a backup receiver and first baseman for the Indians and Phillies from 1903 to 1905.

Bishop could see the ball better than most of his peers; he walked more than 100 times in seven of his twelve seasons (1924–35) for the Athletics and Red Sox while compiling a career batting average of .271 and a lifetime on-base percentage that is just short of .420.

Priest was ordained for the minors after a .174 average in only 9 games for the Yankees in 1911–12.

None of Sexton's four teams (the Mariners, Astros, Athletics, and Cardinals) set about making any bells peal over his .218 average across six seasons in the late 1970s and early 1980s.

Archdeacon administered a shellacking to AL pitching by hitting .333 as a part-time outfielder for the White Sox from 1923 to 1925.

Pope's .265 average, primarily in a backup role, with the Indians and Orioles for four seasons in the 1950s was good but hardly infallible.

Elder didn't put any fannies in the seats with his .250 average in 41 games for the 1949 Browns.

Chaplin didn't have a prayer; he hit only .184 in 35 games as a member of the Red Sox from 1920 to 1922.

Nunn was shipped to a cloister after his 4–3 record and 5.11 ERA for the Cardinals and Reds in three seasons between 1959 and 1962.

Jiggs Parson is in the bullpen.

Harry Shriver is the manager.

Johnny Podres is the pitching coach.

Honorable mention to all the Cardinals of St. Louis and Padres of San Diego.

Could José Pagan make this team? Bless our souls, no.

MAX BISHOP
PHILADELPHIA ATHLETICS – 2ND BASE   1929

Max Bishop was nicknamed Camera Eye for his ability to draw walks.

THE ROYALS

This lineup could become a dynasty.

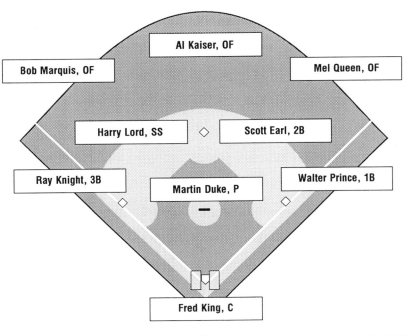

Prince's batting average was a less than princely .208, for four teams in 1883 and 1884.

It doesn't take much time to count Earl's 4 hits for the 1984 Tigers; his average was .114.

Knight performed nobly for the Reds, Mets, and three other teams for thirteen seasons in the 1970s and 1980s; his career mark was .271.

Lord may not have been peerless in his nine major league seasons (1907–15), mostly with the Red Sox and White Sox, but he did hit a creditable .278, primarily as a third baseman but in one game as a shortstop.

Marquis held title to a .273 batting average in 40 games with the 1953 Reds.

Kaiser batted .216 for three teams in three seasons just before World War I.

Queen ruled over very little as either an outfielder (.179) or a pitcher (20–17) for the Reds and Angels from 1964 to 1972.

Ray Knight had the unenviable role of replacing Pete Rose at third base for Cincinnati after the all-time hits leader left the Reds via free agency.

King demonstrated so little that was regal in his 3 hitless at-bats for the AL Milwaukee Brewers in 1901 that he abdicated and assumed the name John Butler for three later seasons with the Cardinals and Dodgers; he improved ever so slightly—to a career average of .134.

Duke's 0–3 record and 7.43 ERA for Washington of the AA in 1891 didn't put him among the mound aristocracy.

Mike Squires, Mike Page, Brett Butler, Bob Usher, Darrell Porter, Pete Coachman, Bob Groom, Smokey Burgess, Jimmy Archer, and Joe Chamberlain would all be around if they were needed. And pitcher Vergil Jester could always be brought into a laugher.

But Joe Tinker and Tom Poorman can't break into this lineup.

Nor would outfielder Art Rebel feel welcome at this team's home park, the Kingdome.

Honorable mention to all the Royals of Kansas City.

THE BEST NAMES

Baseball has had more than its share of colorful names. The following are our choices for the best.

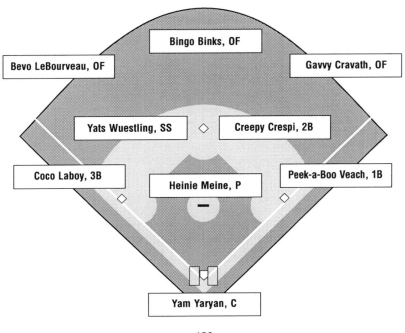

Bingo Binks, OF

Bevo LeBourveau, OF

Gavvy Cravath, OF

Yats Wuestling, SS

Creepy Crespi, 2B

Coco Laboy, 3B

Heinie Meine, P

Peek-a-Boo Veach, 1B

Yam Yaryan, C

William Veach was a .215 hitter for four clubs in three major leagues over three seasons in the 1880s and 1890s.

Frank Angelo Joseph Crespi had a .263 average for the Cardinals from 1938 to 1942; in all but one season (1941), when he was the regular second baseman for St. Louis, he played a utility role.

José Alberto Laboy hit .233 for the Expos from 1969 to 1973. In the club's first season, he hit .258 with 18 homers, but slumped to .199 the following year and was a backup after that.

George Wuestling survived only two seasons (1929 and 1930) with the Tigers and Yankees on his .189 average.

DeWitt Wiley LeBourveau's name was fancier than his stats—.275 in five seasons (1919–1929) with the Phillies and A's.

George Alvin Binkowski stuck around from 1944 to 1948—with the Senators, Athletics, and Browns—by hitting .253.

Clifford Carlton Cravath is the star on this squad. After two nondescript seasons with three AL clubs, he played for the Phillies from 1912 to 1920. He became

Coco Laboy became a fan favorite in Montreal with the field announcer bellowing each syllable of his name with equal emphasis over the public address system.

the most prodigious power hitter in the decade preceding Babe Ruth's move to the outfield, leading the NL in home runs six times and in RBIs twice. His lifetime average was .287.

Clarence Yaryan had a .260 batting average as the White Sox' backup catcher in 1921 and 1922.

Henry Meine compiled a 66–50 record in seven seasons (between 1922 and 1934); the righthander led the NL with 19 wins for the Pirates in 1931.

Honorable mention to Putsy Caballero, Rivington Bisland, Pickles Dilhoeffer, Clyde Kluttz, Boots Poffenberger, Sig Jakucki, Cannonball Titcomb, Emil Bildilli, Garland Buckeye, Pea Ridge Day, Dooley Womack, and the ever-lyrical Van Lingle Mungo.

LETTERS IN THE DIRT

Anyone can devise an All-Star team for each letter of the alphabet, but how about a literally alphabetical lineup?

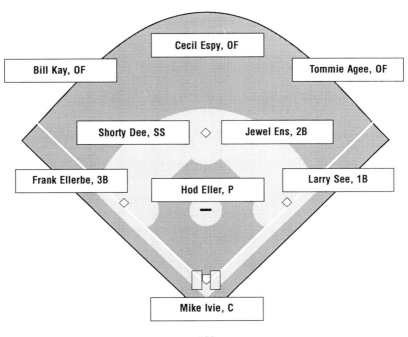

See saw the big leagues twice, each time for only a brief look, and hit only .186 (for the Dodgers in 1986 and the Rangers in 1988).

Ens was a .290 batter in 67 games for the Pirates, from 1922 to 1925.

Ellerbe was almost as well known in his day (1919 to 1924) for being the son of the governor of South Carolina as he was for his .268 average with the Senators, Browns, and Indians.

Dee went 0-for-3 in his only major league game, for the 1915 Browns.

Kay hit .333 in his 25 games for the 1907 Senators.

After eight seasons (in the 1980s and 1990s) Espy had a .244 average with four clubs.

Agee had only a .255 average after twelve seasons (1962–73) with five teams, but he also made two spectacular World Series catches in the same game, for the 1969 Mets.

Mike Ivie showed flashes of excellence at the plate, but he refused to catch and showed no range at either first or third base.

Even though San Diego manager John McNamara once said Ivie "was born to catch," he hated playing the position so much that he once insisted on a clause in his contract specifying that he would not have to go behind the plate. As a consequence, he appeared only nine times as a backstop in his eleven seasons (1971–1983). Despite his lifetime average, for four teams, of .269, Rick Monday once described Ivie as "a forty-million dollar airport with a thirty-dollar control tower."

Eller won 61 games and lost 40, with an impressive 2.62 ERA, for the Reds from 1917 to 1921. He also won 2 games in the tainted 1919 World Series, then later revealed that gamblers had approached him about throwing games against Chicago. Although the righthander reported the approach to manager Pat Moran, his disclosure that *both* teams had been at least initial prey for gamblers was lost in all the publicity surrounding the investigation of the Black Sox.

The bullpen would include Joey Jay and Mark Esser; the bench, Frank Emmer and Roy Ellam. A manager? How about one from Japan? . . . Oh, no. Forget it.

CLOSE BUT NO CIGAR

All of the infielders and outfielders on this team lost batting crowns by less than a point, while the catcher finished a distant third, one and a half points behind the leader, and the pitcher gave up just one run too many to take ERA honors.

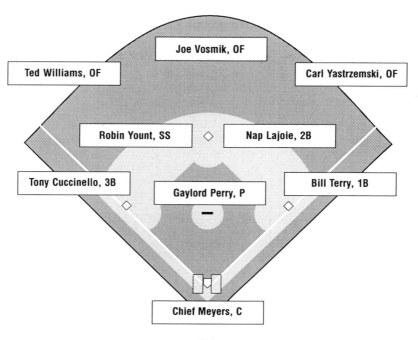

Terry hit .3486 for the 1931 Giants but lost out to Cardinals outfielder Chick Hafey, who finished at .3489; making the race even more interesting was the .3482 average turned in by Hafey's teammate, first baseman Jim Bottomley.

The most contested batting crown belongs to Ty Cobb, who still holds an official edge of just under a point over Lajoie for the 1910 season. The Detroit outfielder earned the honor despite the efforts of Jack O'Connor, the St. Louis Browns' manager, who positioned third baseman Red Corriden to Lajoie's advantage throughout a season-ending doubleheader. However, the result, 6 bunt singles by the Cleveland second baseman, proved insufficient to overtake Cobb, who sat on his .385 average and didn't play in the Tigers' final game. The Chalmers Company, which had offered a new car to the winner, gave automobiles to both future Hall of Famers. There matters rested until 1981, when *Sporting News* researcher Paul MacFarlane rechecked every at-bat by both players in 1910, discovered that one of Cobb's games had been counted twice, calculated that the one-point margin in Cobb's favor was actually a slight deficit, and called for a correction of the historical record. Commissioner Bowie Kuhn refused to consider the case, however, arguing that such a move would open a Pandora's box of requests to revise old statistics.

TONY CUCCINELLO
CINCINNATI REDS – 3RD BASE   1930

When he challenged for the American League batting crown in 1945, Tony Cuccinello hadn't played in more than 40 games in any season since 1940.

The closest batting race ever went to Yankee second baseman Snuffy Stirnweiss for his .309 in 1945. Right behind him (.30854 to .30846) was Chicago's Cuccinello. Two days before the end of the season, the White Sox told the thirty-seven-year-old veteran that he would not be invited back for the 1946 season because they had to make room for players returning from military service.

In 1982, Milwaukee's Yount finished second with .3307 to Willie Wilson's .3316 for the Royals. (Boston rookie Wade Boggs hit .349 but lacked the at-bats to qualify.)

Williams lost in 1949 when his .3428 trailed Detroit third baseman George Kell's .3429. The Red Sox slugger did, however, win six other silver bats.

Vosmik's .3484 average for the 1935 Indians was just shy of second baseman Buddy Myer's .3490 for the Senators.

Yastrzemski's .3286 for the Red Sox in 1970 was lower than outfielder Alex Johnson's .3289 for the Angels.

Playing for the Giants in 1911, Meyers finished third with an average of .3325, which trailed both Honus Wagner's .334 for the Pirates and Doc Miller's .3328 for the Braves.

In the closest contest for ERA honors in history, Perry's 1.916 for the Indians in 1972 was ever so slightly higher than that of Boston's Luis Tiant, who yielded only 1.911 earned runs every 9 innings.

Honorable mention to:

Hal McRae of the 1976 Royals. The DH thought he had the batting crown in hand until the late innings of the final game of the season, when Minnesota outfielder Steve Brye misjudged a fly ball off the bat of George Brett and allowed it to roll to the wall for an inside-the-park home run. When Brett finished at .333 to McRae's .332, the latter exploded, accusing Twins' manager Gene Mauch of having ordered his team to give Brett the edge for racial reasons. While Mauch and Brye both denied the charge, the outfielder did admit later that most AL players wanted Brett to win the title—but only because they didn't believe a DH should win a silver bat.

Teddy Higuera of the 1988 Brewers. The lefthander held the opposition to 2.455 earned runs every 9 innings but lost the title in that category to Allan Anderson of the Twins, whose ERA of 2.446 was marginally lower.

And Sammy Stewart of the 1981 Orioles. What the righthander accomplished on the mound (giving up 29 earned runs in 112 1/3 innings pitched) should have given him an AL-best ERA of 2.323 over Steve McCatty's 2.327 (48 earned runs in 185 2/3 innings pitched)—a slimmer margin than Perry's. But the rules in effect at the time required the rounding off of a hurler's total innings pitched to the highest full number. As a result, McCatty took the honors with a 2.323 to Stewart's 2.330. The rule was changed after the season to include fractions of innings.

Al Rosen cost himself an honorable mention here when he narrowly missed a Triple Crown in 1953 by getting edged out for the batting crown by Mickey Vernon by almost a point and a half—.337 to .3356. In an effort to catch the Washington first baseman, Rosen picked up 3 hits in his season finale but deprived himself of a fourth hit that would have given him the title (by a margin narrower than Stirnweiss's over Cuccinello) when he overran first base without touching the bag. Meanwhile, some faulty dugout arithmetic led Vernon's teammates to the erroneous conclusion that if the first baseman made one more out, the title would go to Rosen. To make sure that didn't happen, catcher Mickey Grasso made sure he was picked off second base after a double and outfielder Kite Thomas conveniently strolled around first base toward second after hitting a single.

Fielder Jones is the manager because his St. Louis Terriers finished second in the closest pennant race in major league history, in the FL in 1915. Joe Tinker's Chicago Whales won the second FL pennant with 86 wins and 66 losses for a .566 percentage; Jones's team ended at 87–67, only one percentage point out of first; and the third-place Pittsburgh Rebels, piloted by Rebel Oakes, were a half game behind with a record of 86 and 67.

On the other hand, the widest disparity between a batting champion's average and that of the second-best hitter was the 75 points that separated Nap Lajoie's AL record .422 for the Athletics in 1901 from Mike Donlin's .347 for the Baltimore Orioles. The biggest margin between the ERAs of the top two pitchers in a league was the 1.18 runs per 9 innings between Greg Maddux's 1.56 for the Braves in 1994 and Bret Saberhagen's 2.74 for the Mets.

REMARKABLE RUNNERS-UP

These players finished second in significant categories despite totals that would have put them first in almost any other season.

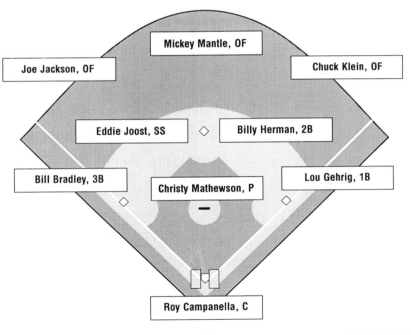

Gehrig's .765 slugging average for the 1927 Yankees was the fourth highest ever. Teammate Babe Ruth holds the top three marks; one was his .772 in 1927.

Only eight players have topped Herman's 57 doubles for the 1936 Cubs. Among them was Joe Medwick of the Cardinals, who set the NL record of 64 two-baggers in the same year.

Only seven times since 1900 has anyone legged out 25 triples in a season. Detroit's Sam Crawford reached that number in 1903, the same year Bradley had three fewer for the Indians.

Joost's 149 walks for the 1949 Athletics rank sixth on the all-time list; that same year, Boston's Ted Williams walked 162 times, the second-highest total in history.

Jackson's .408 (for the 1911 Indians) is the highest second-place batting average of the twentieth century. Even though his percentage is the sixth highest of the century, he was bested by Ty Cobb's .420, the fourth highest. Cobb himself is the only other player to crack the .400 barrier in this century and lose the batting crown; his .401 in 1922 was a distant second to the .420 compiled by George Sisler of the Browns.

BILLY HERMAN
CHICAGO CUBS – 2ND BASE   1932

Billy Herman had back-to-back seasons in which he hit 57 doubles, a figure good enough to lead the NL in 1935, when the runner-up was Joe Medwick.

Mantle's 54 home runs for the 1961 Yankees marked the only time a player slugged as many round-trippers without leading his league. He reached that personal high the same year teammate Roger Maris broke Babe Ruth's record by clouting 61.

The Phillies' Klein takes first place for frustration: In 1930, his 250 hits, one of the six highest totals in history, fell short of Bill Terry's NL record 254 for the Giants, and his 170 RBIs, one of the nine best run-producing seasons, came while Chicago's Hack Wilson was tearing up the record book by driving 190 runs across the plate.

Despite being the only catcher to hit 40 homers in a season (1953), Campanella had to settle for third place in that power category, behind both Eddie Mathews of the Braves (47) and Brooklyn teammate Duke Snider (42).

Mathewson posted back-to-back seasons of 33 and 30 wins for the Giants in 1904 and 1905; teammate Joe McGinnity topped him both years, with totals of 35 and 31.

OUT OF PROPORTION

From a mathematical point of view, these players had some very unlikely achievements.

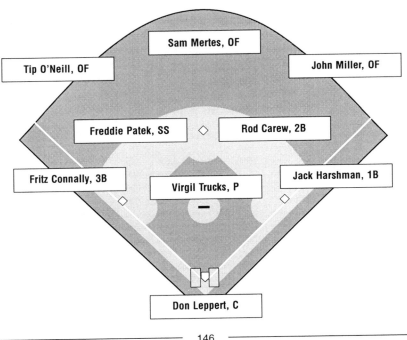

As a pitcher and a first baseman in ten big league seasons (between 1948 and 1960), Harshman had 21 home runs among his 76 hits, the highest ratio of homers to safeties among players with at least 400 at-bats.

Carew stole 19 bases for the Twins in 1969, but 7 of them were of home plate.

In his 58 major league games for the Cubs in 1983 and the Orioles in 1985, Connally hit only 3 home runs, but 2 of them were grand slams.

Patek hit 3 homers in a game on June 20, 1980, but the Angels' shortstop managed only 2 more round-trippers the rest of the season.

In 1887, while with the St. Louis Browns, O'Neill became the only man ever to lead a league in doubles, triples, and homers in the same season; over a ten-year career, he never again finished first in any of these categories. The righthanded hitter had arguably the greatest season in baseball history, topping AA batters in runs, hits, batting, slugging, and on-base percentage as well as extra-base hits.

Freddie Patek on being the shortest player in the major leagues: "It beats being the tallest player in the minor leagues."

There have been only 13 no-hitters broken up in extra innings, and Mertes was the spoiler in two of them. On May 9, 1901, Cleveland righthander Earl Moore held the White Sox hitless through 9 innings, but Mertes started a one-out, game-winning rally with a single in the tenth; Chicago won the game, 4–2, on 2 hits. Three years later, on June 11, Mertes, then with the Giants, singled again in the tenth, this time with two out, to negate Bob Wicker's masterpiece; the base hit was the only one the righthander gave up, and the Cubs scored in the top of the twelfth to win the game. When he wasn't wrecking pitchers' claims to immortality, Mertes was a .279 hitter over ten seasons with five teams.

Miller homered in his first major league at-bat (for the 1966 Yankees) and his last (for the 1969 Dodgers); they were the only round-trippers of his career.

On April 11, 1963, Leppert hit 3 homers in a game for the Senators but only 12 more in his four-year career.

Trucks finished the 1952 season for the Tigers with a 5–19 record, but 2 of the victories were no-hitters, one was a one-hitter, and another was a two-hitter.

JEWISH STARS

In the beginning there was Lip Pike, the first Jewish major leaguer, who joined the NL in its inaugural year of 1876.

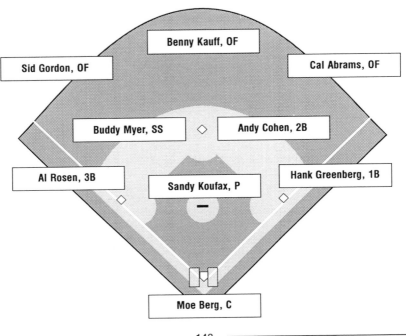

One of the premier power hitters of all time (331 homers in thirteen seasons, between 1930 and 1947, mostly with Detroit), Greenberg was often presumed to be carrying the Jewish people on his shoulders during his career. In 1934 he admitted consulting a rabbi about whether he should take the field on Rosh Hashanah and Yom Kippur in late September. Aware of the pennant race between the Tigers and Yankees, the rabbi compromised, advising Greenberg to play on the happy occasion of Rosh Hashanah but to dedicate himself to prayer on the Day of Atonement. The first baseman complied by hitting a tenth-inning homer on the Jewish New Year to clinch the flag for Detroit and make an appearance on the more solemn holiday unnecessary. By joining the armed services in May 1941, the righthanded slugger became the first American Leaguer to put on a military uniform in the World War II years; in doing so, he made it clear that he considered himself a role model not only for other big leaguers but also for all Jews. When he finally

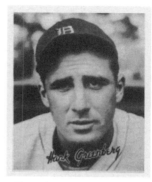

Even though he spent years searching for a Jewish player, Giants manager John McGraw rejected a young Hank Greenberg as too clumsy.

returned, in 1945, it was just in time to nail down another pennant for the Tigers, this time with a grand slam on the final day of the season.

Cohen provided the occasion for one of manager John McGraw's efforts to attract New York's substantial Jewish population to the Polo Grounds. Succeeding Rogers Hornsby at second base for the Giants after the Hall of Famer had been traded to the Braves in 1928, he became a victim of the anti-Hornsby predisposition of the New York press, which jumped all over a few timely April hits by Cohen and began posting daily comparisons of the two second basemen's statistics. Even the usually cantankerous Hornsby was moved to ask the dailies to tone it down. Cohen held down the keystone spot for only two seasons, batting .294 and .274.

Rosen crammed a lot of hitting into his seven full seasons with the Indians (1950–56) as well as parts of the three preceding years. He led the AL in home runs and RBIs twice each, narrowly missing a Triple Crown in 1953 when he lost the batting crown to Mickey Vernon of the Senators by one point. After 1954, injuries sharply curtailed the third baseman's productivity, prompting merciless attacks from Cleveland fans, especially in 1956, when the crowds were whipped up by hints in the press that there was something sinister about a Jewish player being allowed to play through a horrendous slump on a team, one of whose owners, Greenberg, was also a Jew. Rosen retired at the end of the season.

A nearly forgotten place-hitting expert for the Senators and Red Sox from 1925 to 1941, Myer batted .303, including an AL-leading .349 in 1935; he also topped the circuit in stolen bases in 1928. A proficient drag bunter, the infielder once beat out 60 bunts in a season.

Gordon contributed 13 homers to the 1947 Giants' NL record 221 round-trippers. He slugged a total of 202, including five straight seasons with at least 25, in a thirteen-year career between 1941 and 1955. Despite being a favorite among New York's Jewish fans, the outfielder was traded to the Braves after the 1949 season in the deal that brought Alvin Dark and Eddie Stanky to the Polo Grounds.

The Ty Cobb of the Federals, Kauff led the FL in batting in both years of its existence (for the Indianapolis Hoosiers in 1914 and the Newark Peppers in 1915). Otherwise, he was a .311 hitter over eight seasons, primarily with the Giants; his career ended in 1920 when he was banned from baseball by Commissioner Landis after being indicted for—but acquitted of—complicity in an auto-theft operation.

A reserve outfielder for the Boys of Summer Dodgers, Abrams was the goat of the 1950 season for getting thrown out at the plate by Phillies center fielder Richie Ashburn in the ninth inning of the year's final game with what would have been the run that forced a special playoff between Brooklyn and Philadelphia. The lifetime .269 hitter (for five teams from 1949 to 1956) had little choice in trying to score, however, since Pee Wee Reese was right behind him, steaming into third.

The most accomplished backup catcher in major league history, Berg appeared in 100 games only once in his fifteen seasons (between 1923 and 1939) with five clubs; the .243 career hitter was also the subject of Cardinal scout Mike Gonzalez's report that brought the phrase "good field, no hit" into the baseball lexicon. While playing in the big leagues, Berg picked up several advanced degrees, claimed proficiency in Sanskrit and a dozen other languages, and professed to have used the opportunity presented by a 1934 barnstorming trip to take pictures of Tokyo that were later used to plan Gen. Jimmy Doolittle's 1942 air raids on the city. Be that as it may, he did track German nuclear physicists for the OSS during World War II and provided information that may have helped American troops apprehend Werner Heisenberg, the head of Nazi Germany's atomic-bomb project. It was not until the late 1960s that the catcher-turned-spy decided to tell his story, but the book project died aborning when a young editor assigned to the project spent the better part of a preliminary meeting lauding the movies of his prospective author, whom he thought was Moe of the Three Stooges.

The southpaw Koufax is not only the best Jewish pitcher of all time, but also, for the final five of his twelve major league seasons (1955–66), may have been the greatest of all time. In that half-decade, he posted 111 of his 165 wins for the Dodgers, led the NL in shutouts and strikeouts (with 300-plus K's) three times each, and topped the circuit's hurlers in ERA all five years (three times with totals under 2.00). He retired before his thirty-first birthday and, five years later, became the youngest man ever enshrined in Cooperstown.

Pike was not only the first Jewish player in the major leagues, but he also became the first Jewish manager when he took over as pilot for the Reds in 1877.

Honorable mention to two goyim:

Ed Levy, who came to the Yankees in 1942 amid much fanfare designed to bring Jewish fans to the Bronx. What nobody but Levy and New York general manager Ed Barrow knew was that Levy was the name of the first baseman's stepfather, that his real name was Edward Clarence Whitner, and that he had been raised an Irish Catholic. Levy hit .215 over two seasons.

And David Cone, whose Jewish-sounding name combined with his mound skills to make him such a favorite among Jewish Mets fans in the late 1980s and early 1990s that even his protestations that he was a WASP from Kansas City couldn't dissuade doting fathers from hiring him to appear at bar mitzvah parties for their sons.

THE CONTINENTALS

Even easier to assemble than an all-Jewish team is an all-Italian or all-Polish team. But how about a team of immigrants from Europe?

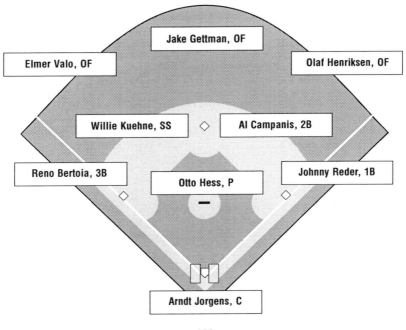

Reder was born in Lublin, Poland; he hit .135 in 17 games for the Red Sox in 1932.

A native of Kos, Greece, Campanis managed only 2 hits in 20 at-bats in his 7 games for the 1943 Dodgers.

Bertoia hailed from St. Vito Udine, Italy; a utility infielder, primarily for the Tigers, from 1953 to 1962, he compiled a .244 average.

Born in Leipzig, Germany, Kuehne had a ten-year big league career (1883–92) in which he hit .232 while playing all over the infield for nine clubs.

Valo came from Ribnik in what was then Czechoslovakia; his twenty-year service in the big leagues (between 1940 and 1961) produced a .282 average. Best remembered as a pinch hitter, he had his best years with the Philadelphia Athletics in the late 1940s and early 1950s, when he topped .300 four times.

Gettman was a native of Frank in what was then, and is once again, Russia. He played for the NL Washington Senators in the final three years of the last century and hit .278.

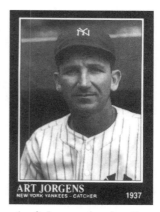

ART JORGENS
NEW YORK YANKEES - CATCHER   1937

Arndt Jorgens played on five pennant-winning Yankee teams but never appeared in a World Series game.

Henriksen left Kirkerup, Denmark, and became a substitute outfielder for the Red Sox from 1911 to 1917; his lifetime average was .269.

Jorgens's birthplace was Modum, Norway. He was a backup for Bill Dickey on the Yankees from 1929 to 1939 and hit .238.

Hess was the best pitcher ever to come out of Berne, Switzerland. The southpaw won 70 and lost 90 for the Indians (1902–08) and Braves (1912–15). He also played some outfield and first base, batting .215 for his career.

Available for bullpen duty are Kurt Krieger of Traisen, Austria (1949 and 1951 Cardinals), and John Michaelson of Taivalkosi, Finland (1921 White Sox).

The bench includes Charlie Bold of Karlskrona, Sweden (1914 Browns); Al Cabrera of the Canary Islands, Spain (1913 Cardinals); and Bruce Bochy of Landes De Bussac, France (three teams for nine seasons in the late 1970s and 1980s).

PACIFIC ISLANDERS

Latin Americans took so enthusiastically to baseball that it is possible to create credible All-Star teams from Puerto Rico, Cuba, the Dominican Republic, Venezuela, Mexico, and Panama. But how about looking west and coming up with one from the Pacific islands?

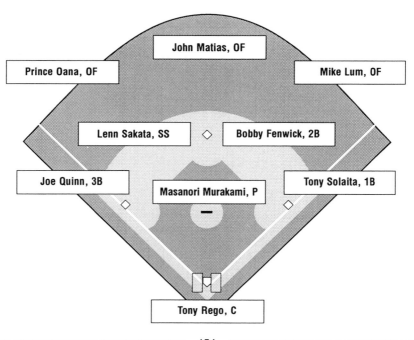

Born in Nuuyli, American Samoa, Solaita learned baseball from GIs. In his seven-season career (between 1968 and 1979), he hit .255 for five clubs.

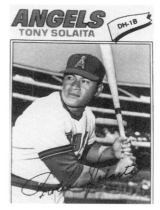

Fenwick played 41 games, for the Astros and Cardinals in 1972 and 1973, and batted an anemic .179. But he is still the best major leaguer born in Naha, Okinawa.

Quinn, who was born in Sydney in 1864, was the first Australian to appear in the major leagues—and the last until the arrival of Craig Shipley in 1986. The infielder bounced around the majors for seventeen seasons (between 1884 and 1901), batting .261.

Sakata, from Honolulu, Hawaii, was a .230-hitting infielder for four clubs from 1977 to 1987, but he entered baseball lore in his only game as a catcher. Put behind the plate by the Orioles in the tenth inning on August 24, 1983, against the Blue Jays, Sakata watched as three successive batters singled off Tippy Martinez, took big leads in anticipation of running on Sakata's untested arm, and got picked off by the southpaw reliever; Sakata later won the game with a home run.

Tony Solaita is the only major leaguer who was born in Polynesia.

Born Henry Kauhane Oana in Waipahu, Hawaii, the Chief played in 6 games as an outfielder with the 1934 Phillies and in 12 as a pitcher–pinch hitter for Detroit in 1943 and 1945. His career average was .308; his mound record, 3–2 (3.77 ERA).

Matias, another Honoluluan, hit .188 in 58 games with the White Sox in 1970.

Lum, yet a third native of Hawaii's largest city, spent fifteen years (1967–81) in the big leagues, most of them with Atlanta. His lifetime average was .247.

Rego, from Wailuku, Hawaii, hit .289 as a backup receiver for the Browns in 1924 and 1925.

Hideo Nomo may be the best Japanese pitcher in the majors, but the pioneer was Murakami. The lefthander had a 5–1 record (3.43 ERA) in 54 appearances for the Giants in 1964 and 1965. He returned to Japan after his father insisted that the honor of the family required that he pitch in his homeland.

Honors to pitcher Chan Ho Park of Kongju City, the only native Korean big leaguer. But not to outfielder Bobby Balcena, who was a California-born Filipino.

VERSATILITY

From the looks of this team it would appear that versatility—at least if defined as appearing in at least 300 games at three different positions—is less a result of fielding skills than of swinging a potent bat while carrying around various gloves. Of course, the DH rule has made candidates for this squad all but obsolete.

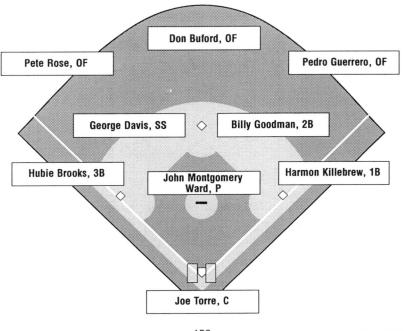

Don Buford, OF

Pete Rose, OF

Pedro Guerrero, OF

George Davis, SS

Billy Goodman, 2B

Hubie Brooks, 3B

John Montgomery Ward, P

Harmon Killebrew, 1B

Joe Torre, C

Killebrew's 573 career homers suggested to a succession of Minnesota managers that they find a place where they could hide his defensive liabilities: Because they kept changing their minds about where that place might be, he played 969 games at first base, 792 at third base, and 470 in the outfield.

Goodman is the only twentieth-century player to win a batting crown while serving as a utility player. In 1950, he led AL hitters with a .354 average for Boston despite playing the outfield (45 games), third base (27), first (21), second (5), short (1), and even pinch-hitting (11). His inability to find a permanent position that year owes much to the fact that the 1950 Red Sox hit .302. (They were the last team to reach a collective .300.) Eight players topped that mark, and the two regulars who finished in the .290s drove in at least 120 runs. In only four of his sixteen major league seasons did Goodman squeeze in as many as 117 games at one spot on the diamond: Boston always

Pete Rose had two obsessions—statistics and gambling; the former helped him achieve the all-time hit record, the latter kept him out of the Hall of Fame.

seemed to have on hand more than enough infielders who were either as good as he was with a bat or better with a glove. His career totals at his three most frequented positions are second base, 624 games; first base, 406, and third base, 330.

As much as anyone else in this lineup, Brooks played his three positions sequentially. He was a third baseman (516 games) for the Mets in the early 1980s. Traded to Montreal in 1985, he became the Expos' shortstop (371 games) for three years, but too many errors and aging legs dictated his being moved to the outfield (542 games) in 1988.

Davis took several seasons before he settled in as a regular shortstop (1,378 games) for the Giants (in 1897) and later the White Sox; most of his 530 games at third base and all of his 303 in the outfield came before then.

Rose is the only player to appear in 300 or more games at four different positions; he was an outfielder 1,327 times, a first baseman in 939 games, a third baseman for 634 contests, and a second baseman on 628 occasions. After starting his career at second, the switch hitter moved to the outfield in 1967, when the arrival of Lee May to play first necessitated Tony Perez's shift to third, which, in turn, pushed Tommy Helms over to second. In 1975, with Ken Griffey ready to play in the outfield every day, Rose moved to third base, with incumbent Dan Driessen relegated to a utility role. When he signed with the Phillies in 1979, Rose became a first baseman because someone named Mike Schmidt already had a lock on the hot corner.

Buford was primarily an infielder (392 games at second and 352 at third) with the White Sox from 1963 to 1967. In Baltimore, for the final five seasons of his ten-year career, he was almost exclusively an outfielder (555 games) because Davey Johnson and Brooks Robinson were fixtures at second and third, respectively.

Guerrero was an outfielder for the Dodgers in the late 1970s and early 1980s, succeeded Ron Cey at third for a few seasons, went back to the outfield for a few more, and settled his fragile legs at first after he moved to the Cardinals in mid-1988. His career totals: outfield, 541 games; first base, 573; and third base, 373.

Torre was a catcher (903 games) for the Braves in both Milwaukee and Atlanta. But after going to the Cardinals in 1969 and on to the Mets in 1975, the righty slugger was compelled to move back and forth between first base (787 contests) and third base (515) because of the presence of Tim McCarver and then Ted Simmons in St. Louis and of Jerry Grote in New York.

A sore arm left Ward with only 291 mound appearances, but his mobility is impressive enough as it stands. He was one of the NL's premier pitchers from 1878 to 1880, winning as many as 47 games in a season and hurling the major leagues' second perfect game. After a detour to the outfield, he became the Giants' shortstop (826) in the 1880s and ended his career in 1894 as a second baseman (491).

Honorable mention to the other three 300/300/300 players:

Buck Herzog: 488 games at second base, 472 at third, and 458 at short for the Giants, Braves, Reds, and Cubs from 1908 to 1920;

Pete Runnels: 644 games as a first baseman, 642 as a second baseman, and 463 as a shortstop for the Senators, Red Sox, and Astros from 1951 to 1964;

And Derrell Thomas: 608 games at second, 542 in the outfield, and even though he never played the position more than 74 times in any one season, 339 at short for the Astros, Padres, Giants, Dodgers, Expos, Angels, and Phillies from 1971 to 1985.

Aside from Rose, Denis Menke is the only player in the history of the game to hold down, in one season or another, a regular lineup spot (defined as 100 or more games) at four different positions. He was primarily a shortstop—for the Braves in both Milwaukee (1964) and Atlanta (1966–67) and for the Astros (1969–70). But he also served as Houston's second baseman (1968) and first baseman (1971) and Cincinnati's third baseman (1972–73).

Also with the exception of Rose, Honus Wagner is the only player to appear in as many as 200 games at four different positions in his career. Aside from shortstop (1,888 games), he was also at various times an outfielder (372), first baseman (248), and third baseman (209) for Louisville and Pittsburgh from 1897 to 1917.

Even more rare than the triple-300 threats are those players who appeared in at least 1,000 games at two positions:

In his twenty-two seasons (between 1941 and 1963) with the Cardinals, Stan Musial appeared in 1,896 games in the outfield and 1,016 at first base.

Ernie Banks was the Cubs' shortstop for 1,125 games, from 1953 to 1961, and a first baseman for the same club for 1,259 contests, from 1962 to 1971.

Ron Fairly moved back and forth between first base (1,218 games) and the outfield (1,037 games) for the Dodgers, the Expos, and four other clubs, from 1958 to 1978.

Rod Carew started his career as Minnesota's second baseman in 1967 and played 1,130 contests at that position; in 1976, he moved to first base, where he had 1,184 appearances for both Minnesota and, from 1979 until his retirement in 1985, California.

Robin Yount was Milwaukee's shortstop for 1,479 contests from 1974 to 1984, then moved to the outfield, where he played 1,218 games through 1992.

STAYING PUT

On the other hand, these are the players who appeared in the most games at their positions without ever filling in anywhere else.

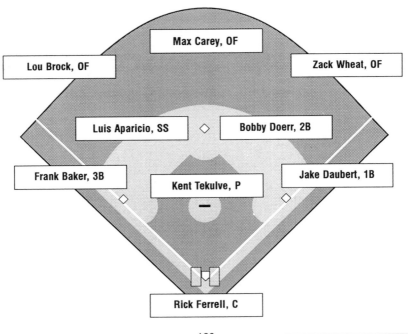

Daubert held down first for 2,001 games for the Dodgers and Reds from 1910 to 1924. He hit .303.

Doerr played only second in his 1,852 contests, and only for the Red Sox, to establish a record for permanence for one team at one position. The lifetime .288 hitter clouted 223 homers and drove in 100 runs six times in his fourteen seasons (between 1937 and 1951).

Baker's 1,548 games at third were for the Athletics (1908–14) and Yankees (1916–19 and 1921–22). He led the AL in homers four times and hit .307.

Aparicio's 2,581 games at short (for the White Sox, Orioles, and Red Sox from 1956 to 1973) are a record for players who appeared at only one diamond spot. Playing in at least 109 games in each of his eighteen seasons, he topped the AL in stolen bases in his first nine seasons while batting .262 for his career.

Brock played the most games exclusively as an outfielder, 2,507 for the Cubs and Cardinals from 1961 to 1979. The .293 hitter is second on the all-time stolen-base list with 938.

Carey led the NL in steals ten times in twenty seasons (1910–29) with the Pirates and Dodgers; his name was penciled in as an outfielder 2,422 times.

Although he spent most of his career in Ted Williams's shadow, Bobby Doerr was always singled out by Williams as the indispensable Boston player of the 1940s.

Wheat, a .317 hitter from 1909 to 1917, appeared in the pasture 2,350 times. Except for his final season with the Athletics, the lefty batter was a Brooklyn Dodger.

Ferrell bounced around among the Browns, the Senators, and the Red Sox for eighteen years between 1929 and 1947, batting .281 while catching 1,806 games.

Tekulve's 1,050 relief appearances are the most games without a starting assignment. His record, from 1974 to 1989 with the Pirates and two other NL teams, is 94–90, 184 saves, and a 2.85 ERA in only 1,436 innings.

The pilot with the most longevity was Connie Mack; his fifty-three years as a dugout boss included three with the Pirates (1894–96) and fifty with the Athletics (1901–50).

Full honors in waiting to Ozzie Smith, who, unless he gets it into his head to bring his glove somewhere else on the field, should pass Aparicio's mark in 1996.

TEMPORARY RELIEF

Some surprising people took a turn or two—or more—on the mound.

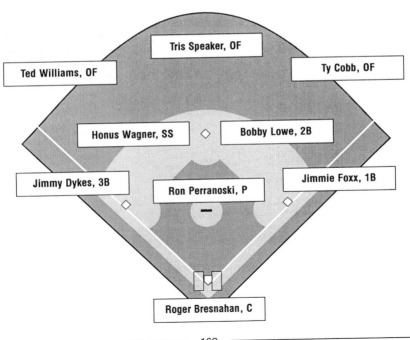

While moundsman Foxx didn't make anyone forget first baseman Foxx's slugging, he did fashion a 1.52 ERA in 23 2/3 innings over ten appearances (one for the Red Sox in 1939 and nine for the Phillies in 1945), including two starts. His career record was 1–0.

Lowe is best remembered as the first player to clout 4 home runs in a game (on May 30, 1894, for the Braves); on the other hand, in his only inning as a pitcher (in 1891 for Boston) he gave up 3 hits and one run for a 9.00 ERA.

It took Dykes 2 innings, in 2 different games for the 1927 Athletics, to surrender a run for a 4.50 ERA.

Wagner took the mound twice (once each in 1900 and 1902) for the Pirates and emerged without giving up an earned run; in 8 1/3 innings he yielded 7 hits and 6 walks but also struck out 6 batters.

Williams, who always claimed that all pitchers are stupid, took a turn at trying to get other batters out. In two innings for the 1940 Red Sox, he gave up a run on 3 hits (4.50 ERA); of the nine batters he faced, one struck out and two bounced back to the box.

Tris Speaker's lifetime 792 doubles are the most by a major leaguer.

Speaker's mound career consisted of one inning for the 1914 Red Sox in which he gave up a run on 2 hits.

Cobb's 5 innings (in 2 games in 1918 and one in 1925, all for the Tigers) produced a 3.60 ERA but no decisions; he did, however, earn a save in his final appearance in the box, when player-manager Cobb brought outfielder Cobb in to pitch an inning and retire the side in order.

Bresnahan started 6 games (5 for Washington of the NL in 1897 and one for the AL Baltimore Orioles in 1901) and relieved in 3 others (once each for the Senators, the Orioles, and in 1910, the Cardinals). He completed 3 of his starts, posted a 4–1 record, and retired with a .3.93 ERA.

Perranoski started in only one of his 737 games on the mound. The southpaw bullpen ace for the Dodgers, Twins, and others led the NL in appearances three times and the AL in saves twice between 1961 and 1973.

CONSECUTIVE-GAME STREAKS

Everyone in North America knows that, in 1995, Cal Ripken topped Lou Gehrig's streak of 2,130 consecutive games played. What is not so well known is that Ripken had a more impressive streak broken seven years before he topped Gehrig. The members of this team played the most consecutive games at their respective positions.

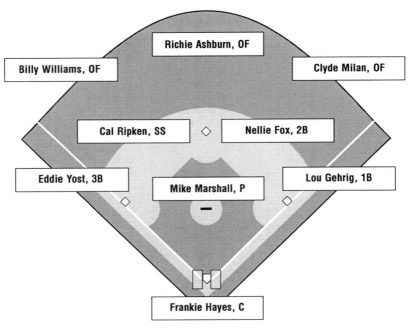

Richie Ashburn, OF

Billy Williams, OF

Clyde Milan, OF

Cal Ripken, SS

Nellie Fox, 2B

Eddie Yost, 3B

Lou Gehrig, 1B

Mike Marshall, P

Frankie Hayes, C

Gehrig's longest streak at first base lasted 885 games, from the day he took over for Wally Pipp until the last game of the 1930 season, when he played the outfield. The following year, he began another streak at first that would have exceeded the earlier one but for a 1934 road game when he was inserted into the lineup as the shortstop and leadoff hitter—long enough to single and retire for a pinch runner.

Fox's streak of 798 games for the White Sox lasted from 1955 to 1960.

Yost kept going, for the Senators, for 576 games (1951–55) at third base and for 829 contests, including pinch-hitting and outfield appearances.

Ripken ended the 1995 season having played 2,126 consecutive games at shortstop and 2,153 overall. Even more remarkable is that Ripken played every inning of every game from June 5, 1982, through September 14, 1987—a total of 8,243 frames over 904 games—until he was removed in mid-game by his father, then managing the Orioles.

Williams appeared as an outfielder for the Cubs in 897 consecutive contests (1963–69); including pinch-hitting assignments, the streak lasted 1,117 games.

FRANKIE HAYES
PHILADELPHIA ATHLETICS – CATCHER   1934

In 1946, Frankie Hayes was Bob Feller's batterymate for an April no-hitter; after a trade to the White Sox, the catcher broke up the righthander's bid for another no-hitter, in August.

Ashburn's outfield streak lasted 694 games, for the Phillies, from 1950 to 1954; with pinch-hitting appearances, he appeared in 730 straight contests.

No AL outfielder has surpassed Milan's 511 consecutive games between 1910 and 1913 for the Senators.

Hayes's mark is 312 games. The receiver was with the Browns at the end of 1943 when the streak began, the Athletics in 1944 and part of 1945, and the Indians for part of 1945 and the beginning of 1946 when it came to a close.

Marshall relieved in 13 straight games for the Dodgers, in June and July 1974.

Others with 1,000-game streaks are shortstop Everett Scott, 1,307 (1916–25, Red Sox and Yankees); first baseman Steve Garvey, 1,207, including pinch-hitting appearances, (1975–83, Dodgers and Padres); and shortstop–third baseman Joe Sewell, 1,103 (1922–30, Indians). Dale Mohorcic of the Rangers tied Marshall's streak in 1986.

CONSECUTIVE ERRORLESS GAMES

These players appeared in the most consecutive games without making an error.

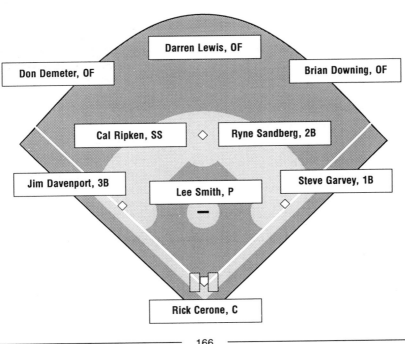

Darren Lewis, OF

Don Demeter, OF

Brian Downing, OF

Cal Ripken, SS

Ryne Sandberg, 2B

Jim Davenport, 3B

Lee Smith, P

Steve Garvey, 1B

Rick Cerone, C

Garvey's streak of 193 errorless games began in his first year with the Padres, the same season his string of consecutive games ended, and extended into 1985.

Sandberg's 123 games, for the Cubs, stretched over the 1989 and 1990 seasons.

It took Davenport half of 1966, all of 1967, and the beginning of 1968 to put together a string of 97 games without a miscue. During that time he also played second base and shortstop for the Giants.

Ripken's 95 straight games of flawless fielding for the Orioles were all in 1990.

Lewis's 392 straight games without a misplay began in 1990, when he was with Oakland, and didn't end until 1994, several years after he had crossed the Bay to play for San Francisco. His is the longest streak among position players, and he did it playing an aggressive center field and finishing near the league leaders in putouts in 1993 and 1994.

When Demeter wasn't playing first base or third for the Phillies in 1962 and 1963 or stationed at first for the Tigers in 1964 and 1965, he was in the outfield for 266 games without committing a misplay.

Darren Lewis committed nine errors in two-and-a-half minor league seasons but only eight in six years in the major leagues.

Originally a catcher, Downing was on his way to becoming the Angels' DH when he put together his AL record streak for an outfielder of 244 games (1981–83).

Cerone began his streak with the Yankees in 1987; two years later, when he made his first error in 159 games, he was a member of the Red Sox.

Smith made 546 appearances over more than a decade without a fielding lapse. His skein extended from 1982 to 1992; in that time the righthander pitched for the Cubs, Red Sox, and Cardinals.

In a lineup based on consecutive fielding chances without an error, only Sandberg (577 chances), Ripken (431), and Lewis (938) would be repeaters. Their teammates would be Stuffy McInnis (1,700 to Garvey's 1,633) at first, Don Money (261 to Davenport's 209) at third, Ken Griffey Jr. (573) and Curt Flood (568) over Downing (471) and Demeter (449) in the outfield, Yogi Berra (950 to Cerone's 896), and Claude Passeau (273 to reliever Smith's mere 93).

BEST CAREER LEAGUE CHAMPIONSHIP SERIES

A lineup of players who always showed that little extra effort when they were within reach of a pennant.

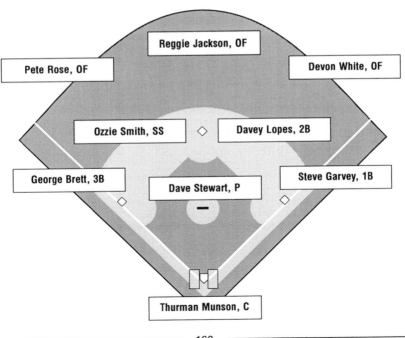

Garvey collected 8 homers to go with a .356 batting average and 21 RBIs in 22 games over four League Championship Series (LCS) with the Dodgers (1974, 1977, 1978, and 1981) and one with the Padres (1984).

Lopes stole 9 bases while hitting a solid .282 as Garvey's Los Angeles teammate in four postseason championships, plus one each with the Cubs (1984) and Astros (1986).

The premier playoff player, Brett swatted a record 9 homers and 4 triples to go with a batting average of .340 and a slugging mark of .728. All six of his LCS appearances were with the Royals (1976–78, 1980, and 1984–85).

Smith batted .351 to lead St. Louis into three World Series (in 1982, 1985, and 1987).

Rose batted .381 in his seven LCS, five with the Reds (1970, 1972–73, 1975–76) and two with the Phillies (1980 and 1983).

In addition to his LCS heroics, George Brett hit .373 in two World Series.

Jackson hit 6 homers and 7 doubles, scored 16 runs, and drove in 20 despite a .227 batting average in his record eleven LCS appearances (five straight for the A's from 1971 to 1975, four with the Yankees in 1977–78 and 1980–81, and two with the Angels in 1982 and 1986).

White's .392 is the highest batting average in LCS history for players with at least 50 at-bats. He reached that figure over four Series, one with California (1986) and three with Toronto (1991–93).

Munson batted .339 with 10 RBIs in 14 games for the Yankees (1976–78).

Stewart won 8 LCS games without a loss while compiling a 2.03 ERA for Oakland (1988–90 and 1992) and Toronto (1993). (Curiously, the righthander compiled a 40.50 ERA and lost 2 games for the Dodgers in the 1981 split-season playoffs, and in World Series competition he had a 2–5 record.)

The manager should be either Sparky Anderson for his five LCS victories (1970, 1972, and 1975–76 Reds; 1984 Tigers) despite his two losses, or Tom Kelly for his perfect record in LCS competition (with the 1987 and 1991 Twins).

BEST LEAGUE CHAMPIONSHIP SERIES

What is most surprising about this team is that not all of its players went on to the World Series.

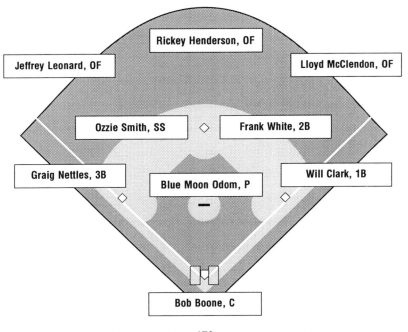

Clark hit .650 (13-for-20), with 2 homers, 3 doubles, a triple, 8 RBIs, and 8 runs scored to lead the Giants to the 1989 pennant over the Cubs in 5 games.

White went 6-for-11 (.545) in the Royals' 3-game sweep of the Yankees in 1980.

Nettles's contribution to the Yankees' 3-game sweep of the Athletics the following year was a .500 average with 9 RBIs.

Smith, proving as deft with a bat as with his glove, defeated the Dodgers in one game with his first big league homer from the left side and batted .435 in 6 games for the pennant-winning 1985 Cardinals.

Leonard's 4 homers and .417 batting average were good enough to win him the 1987 series MVP even though the Giants lost to the Cardinals in 7 games.

Henderson devastated the Blue Jays in 1989 with a double, a triple, 2 homers, 8 runs scored, 5 RBIs, 7 walks, and 8 stolen bases; his batting average for the A's was .400, his slugging percentage 1.000, and his on-base percentage .590 as Oakland took the AL flag in 5 games.

Lloyd McClendon hinted at what was to come when he collected two hits in three at-bats in the 1989 LCS for the Cubs.

It certainly wasn't McClendon's fault that the Pirates lost the 1992 LCS to the Braves. The outfielder collected 8 hits in 11 at-bats for a .727 average. Two of the hits were doubles, and one was a home run, giving him a 1.182 slugging percentage. He also walked four times for an .800 on-base percentage. Most surprising is that he appeared in only 5 of the 7 games.

Boone couldn't get California past Boston in 1986 despite going 10-for-22 (.455) in 7 games.

Odom started 2 games for Oakland in 1972, completed one, won both, scattered 5 hits, and yielded no earned runs in 14 innings as the A's beat the Tigers in 5 games.

Honorable mention to Terry Puhl (1980 Astros) for going 10-for-19 (.526); Fred Lynn (1982 Angels) for his 11-for-18 (.611); Lynn's teammate Don Baylor for 10 RBIs in 5 games; and Mark Grace (1989 Cubs) for his 11-for-17 (.647) with 8 RBIs.

BEST LEAGUE CHAMPIONSHIP GAME

Nobody has hit 4 home runs or pitched a no-hitter in the LCS yet, but in the meantime:

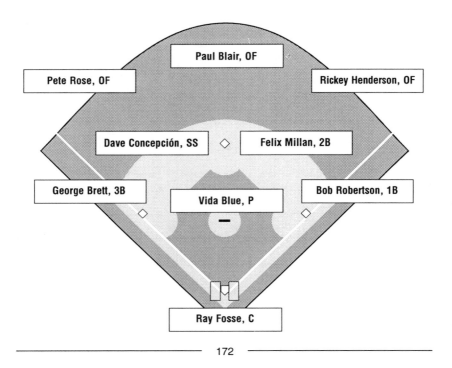

Robertson went 4-for-5 with 3 homers and a double and drove home 5 runs to lead the Pirates to a win over the Giants in Game 2 of the 1971 National League LCS.

Millan reached base in all five of his plate appearances for the Braves in Game 2 of the first NLCS, in 1969; he had 2 singles and 3 walks in a losing effort to the Mets.

Brett's 3 solo homers for the Royals didn't stop the Yankees from taking Game 3 of the 1978 American League Series.

Concepción boosted the Reds over the Pirates in the second game of the 1975 NLCS with 3 singles in 4 at-bats, a pair of stolen bases, and several flashy fielding plays.

Blair clobbered Minnesota pitching for 5 hits (including a homer and 2 doubles) and drove in 5 runs for the victorious Orioles in the third game of the first ALCS, in 1969; no one else in either league has had as many safeties in a single LCS game.

Rose's twelfth inning homer in the fourth game of the 1973 Series not only capped a 3-hit performance by the switch hitter and gave the Reds a victory over the Mets, but the blow also came a day after Shea Stadium fans almost rioted because of Rose's rough slide into Bud Harrelson.

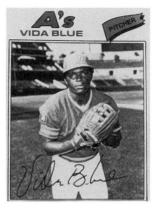

Vida Blue's masterpiece for the A's in the 1974 LCS was the only postseason game he ever won; he had two losses in his other eight LCS games and lost all three of his World Series decisions in eight appearances.

Henderson set the pace for Oakland's 1989 defeat of Toronto by stroking two singles in his 2 at-bats, walking in his other 2 plate appearances, scoring 2 runs, and stealing an LCS record 4 bases in Game 2 of the AL series.

Fosse went 3-for-4 with a double and a homer and 3 RBIs to lead Oakland to a win over the Orioles in the second game of the 1974 ALCS.

Blue yielded only 2 hits, walked none, and struck out 7 in a 1–0 victory over Baltimore in Game 3 of the same 1974 series.

WORST CAREER LEAGUE CHAMPIONSHIP SERIES

Each of these players had at least 20 swings, but none of them did much to help his team move on to the World Series.

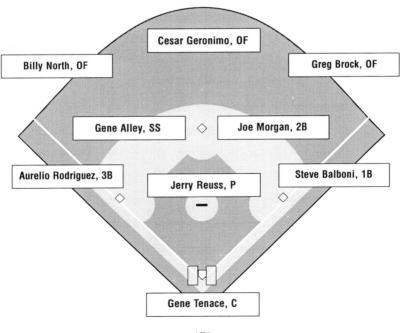

Balboni was a mere 4-for-35 (.114) and drove in only one run for the Royals in 1984 and 1985.

The biggest surprise member of this squad is Morgan. Despite his reputation as Mr. Clutch, he hit only .135 (13-for-96) with a scant 5 RBIs in seven LCS (1972–73, 1975–76, and 1979 for the Reds; 1980 for the Astros; and 1983 for the Phillies).

Rodriguez managed only 2 hits in 22 at-bats for a meager .091 average over four series (1972 Tigers, 1980–81 Yankees, and 1983 White Sox).

Alley's 1-for-25 (.040) for the Pirates in 1970, 1971, and 1972 stood as the single worst LCS effort—but only briefly.

North almost made Alley look good by going 1-for-34 (.029) with the Athletics in 1974 and 1975 and the Dodgers in 1978.

Geronimo was only relatively more reliable with his 6-for-63 (.095) as Morgan's teammate on five Cincinnati Western Division winners.

And Brock gave Alley and North a run for their money by going 1-for-21 (.048) for the Dodgers in 1983 and 1985, even though his only hit was a home run.

Joe Morgan hit a home run in his first two LCS games, in 1972, and never hit another in 25 more National League Championship contests.

Although he is associated with World Series slugging, Tenace didn't do much to help the Athletics get to the Fall Classic—going only 5-for-57 (.088) and driving home only two runs over five consecutive ALCS (1971–75).

Southpaw Reuss compiled a record of 0–7, with an ERA of 5.45 in 33 innings, for the Pirates (1974–75) and Dodgers (1981, 1983, and 1985).

Danny Ozark (1976–78 Phillies) and Jim Leyland (1990–92 Pirates) share the dubious honor of calling the shots for this team. Each of them lost three straight LCS without ever winning one.

Runners-up include Mookie Wilson (12-for-66, .182), Dave Parker (11-for-58, .190), John Milner (3-for-27, .111), and Doyle Alexander (0–4, 8.61 ERA in 23 innings).

BEST CAREER WORLD SERIES

Reggie Jackson hasn't been the only Mr. October, not even for the Yankees.

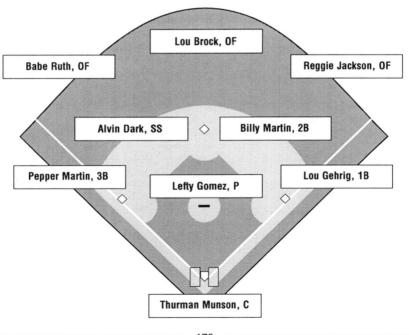

Gehrig hit .361 with 10 homers, 35 RBIs, and a .731 slugging percentage for seven Yankee World Series entries (1926–28, 1932, and 1936–38).

In five Series (1951–53 and 1955–56), all with the Yankees, Billy Martin batted .333 (76 points above his career average), including 5 homers and 19 RBIs.

In three World Series for the Cardinals (1928, 1931, and 1934), Pepper Martin stole 7 bases and compiled a Series-record average of .418 (23-for-55).

Dark's .323 batting average is the best for shortstops who have appeared in three or more World Series; he played for the 1948 Braves and for the 1951 and 1954 Giants.

Ruth's .326 average included 15 homers, 33 RBIs, and a .744 slugging percentage. The Babe did most of this damage to NL pitchers for the Yankees (1921–23, 1926–28, and 1932). In three earlier Series with the Red Sox (1915–16 and 1918), he also had a 3–0 pitching record with a miserly ERA of 0.87.

Brock has the highest batting average (.391) among players with at least 75 World Series at-bats and is tied for the most stolen bases (14). He appeared in three Series (1964, 1967–68) for the Cardinals.

PEPPER MARTIN
INNOCENT AS A BABY   1938

St. Louis general manager Branch Rickey nicknamed Pepper Martin the Wild Horse of the Osage in a superfluous effort to add more color to the Gas House Gang Cardinals of the 1930s.

In two Series with the A's (1973–74) and three with the Yankees (1977–78 and 1981), Mr. October slugged a record .755; his .357 batting average included 10 homers.

In three Series (1976–78) for the Yankees, Munson hit .373 and drove in 12 runs.

Gomez's 6 victories are the most without a World Series loss. He pitched for the Yankees in the 1932 and 1936–39 Series and put together a 2.86 ERA.

Honorable mention to Mickey Mantle of the Yankees for his Series record 18 homers (despite a .257 average); Whitey Ford of the Yankees for his record 10 wins (but not for his record 8 losses); and Jack Billingham of the Reds for his 0.36 ERA, the lowest in Series history (one earned run in 25 1/3 innings of work in 1972 and 1975–76).

Joe McCarthy gets to manage this squad on the basis of his 7 Series victories as opposed to only 2 losses. (Casey Stengel also managed seven world championship clubs, but he lost three times.)

BEST WORLD SERIES

The players in this lineup turned in the most memorable performances in a single World Series.

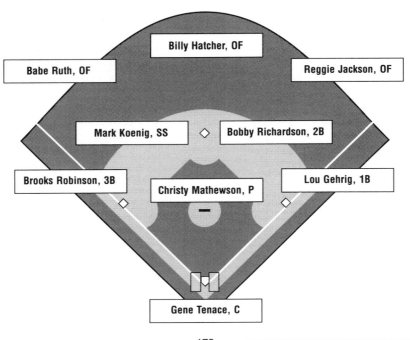

Gehrig devastated the Cardinals for the Yankees in 1928 with his record 1.727 slugging average on 6 doubles, a triple, and 4 homers, good for 9 RBIs and a .545 batting average in only 4 games.

Richardson contributed a .367 average (11-for-30) and a Series-record 12 RBIs to the Yankees' losing effort against the Pirates in 1960; the second baseman also holds the record for most hits in a series—13 in 1964.

Robinson not only turned singles into outs and doubles into double plays in the most impressive post-season defensive exhibition ever by a third baseman; he also ended up with a .429 average and a 5-game-Series-record 17 total bases as the Orioles defeated the Reds in 1970.

Although overshadowed by the slugging of teammates Ruth and Gehrig, Koenig's club-high .500 average and 5 runs scored helped the Yankees sweep the Pirates in 1927.

In 1928, Ruth finished just behind Gehrig in slugging with a 1.375 percentage but ahead of him with a .625 batting average, including 3 homers, in a sweep of the Cardinals.

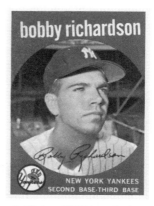

bobby richardson

NEW YORK YANKEES
SECOND BASE-THIRD BASE

A lifetime .266 hitter during the regular season, Bobby Richardson batted .305 in seven World Series.

Jackson's Series-record 5 home runs, .450 batting average, and 1.250 slugging percentage contributed to New York's 6-game victory over the Dodgers in 1977.

Hatcher broke most existing offensive records for a 4-game Series when he led Cincinnati over Oakland in 1990 with 4 doubles and a triple among his 9 hits in 12 official at-bats (.750 and 1.250 batting and slugging averages, respectively), plus two walks and a hit-by-pitch (for an .824 on-base percentage).

A backup catcher for the A's during the 1972 season, Tenace hit only 5 homers while batting .225. In 7 World Series games against the Reds, however, he responded with a .348 average, 5 round-trippers among his 8 hits, and 9 RBIs.

Nobody has ever come close to matching the 3 shutouts Mathewson tossed for the Giants against the Athletics in 1905. In the 27 innings he pitched in six days, the righthander gave up 14 hits and only one walk while striking out 18.

BEST WORLD SERIES GAME

The players in this entry rose to the heights of the heights in one game.

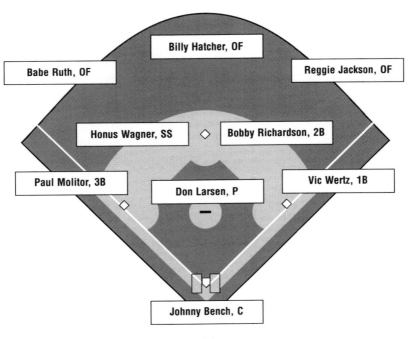

Everyone remembers Willie Mays's great catch against Vic Wertz in the opening game of the 1954 Series; what many may not recall is that the drive was the Cleveland first baseman's bid for a fifth hit in the contest, eventually lost by the Indians.

In the third game against the Pirates in 1960, Richardson knocked in a Series-record 6 runs for the Yankees.

Molitor is the only one to accomplish what Mays prevented Wertz from doing: getting 5 hits in a World Series game. The Milwaukee leadoff batter singled in all but one of his at-bats to set the table for a 10–0 romp over the Cardinals in the first game in 1982.

In Game 3 of the 1909 Series, Wagner had 3 hits, 3 stolen bases, and 3 RBIs to help turn the tide for the Pirates against the Tigers.

Twice Ruth hit 3 homers in a Series game—in the fourth contest of both the 1926 and 1928 Series. On the earlier occasion, he drove in 5 runs and scored 4; on the later one, he had 3 RBIs and 3 runs scored. The Yankees defeated the Cardinals in both instances.

HONUS WAGNER
A WONDERFUL MAN, HE WAS   1914

In the only matchup of their careers, in the 1909 World Series, Honus Wagner outhit Ty Cobb .333 to .231 and stole six bases to his American League rival's two.

Jackson is the only player to match Ruth's one-game total, bashing his 3 homers on three consecutive pitches delivered by three different Dodger pitchers in the sixth and final game of the 1977 Series.

Hatcher picked up 4 hits in the second game of the 1990 series to extend his consecutive hit mark to 7 and to send the Reds rushing toward their sweep of the Athletics.

Bench helped complete a 4-game sweep of the Yankees in 1976 with 2 homers and 5 RBIs.

And anyone who doesn't know about Larsen's fifth-contest perfect game against the Dodgers in 1956 probably should either be reading another book or boning up on the history of the Yankees.

WORST WORLD SERIES CAREER

The position players on this team, whatever their other accomplishments, each had at least 50 World Series at-bats and yet failed to reach the .200 mark.

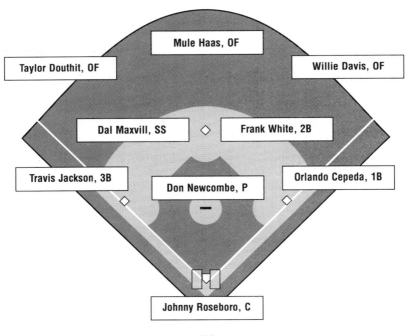

Mule Haas, OF

Taylor Douthit, OF

Willie Davis, OF

Dal Maxvill, SS

Frank White, 2B

Travis Jackson, 3B

Don Newcombe, P

Orlando Cepeda, 1B

Johnny Roseboro, C

Cepeda was only 13-for-76 (.171) with 2 homers and 9 RBIs for the 1962 Giants and 1967–68 Cardinals.

White was 9-for-53 (.170), with a home run and 6 RBIs, for the Royals in 1980 and 1985.

Hall of Famer Jackson, who played more third base than his usual shortstop in Series competition, was a mere 10-for-67 (.149) and made 7 errors, for an .891 fielding percentage in four Series (1923–24, 1933, and 1936) for the Giants.

Maxvill, a candidate for baseball's worst hitter of all time, remained true to form in four Octobers (1964 and 1967–68 with the Cardinals and 1974 with the Athletics), with his 7-for-61 (.115) and only 2 RBIs.

Douthit had only 7 hits in 50 at-bats (.140), including a home run and 3 RBIs over three Series (1926, 1928, and 1930) with the Cardinals.

Haas went 10-for-62 (.161) for the great Athletics' teams of 1929–31; he did, however, hit 2 homers and drive in 9 runs.

Davis contributed little to the Dodgers' effort in the 1963 and 1965–66 Series, collecting only 9 hits in 54 at-bats (.167) and a mere 3 RBIs.

Roseboro could do no better than 11-for-70 (.157), with a homer and 7 RBIs, for the Dodgers in 1959, 1963, and 1965–66.

TRAVIS JACKSON
NEW YORK GIANTS – SHORTSTOP   1924

Travis Jackson was so popular during his years with the Giants that even Dodger fans exempted him from the catcalls that welcomed every other Polo Grounder.

Although several pitchers have lost more World Series games than Newcombe, they also won more and had significantly lower ERAs: Newcombe's career numbers were an 0–4 record and an 8.59 ERA.

Among other anemic World Series hitters were Dave Bancroft (16-for-93, .172), Max Bishop (12-for-66, .182, without an extra-base hit), Frankie Crosetti (20-for-115, .174), and Jimmy Sheckard (14-for-77, .182).

Worse than anemic was Billy Sullivan's 0-for-21 in his only Series, with the White Sox in 1906. And the very worst Fall Classic pitcher was the Yankees' Rip Collins, who gave up 4 earned runs in his two-thirds of a World Series inning (a 54.00 ERA) in 1921.

WORST WORLD SERIES

Sometimes even the most dependable player can't do anything right in the fall.

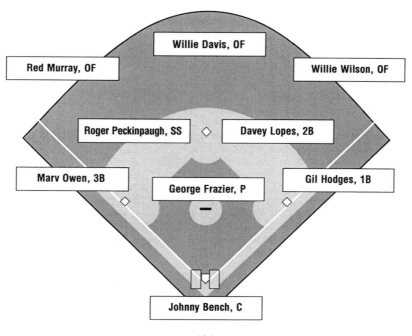

After a season in which he clouted 32 homers and drove in 102 runs for Brooklyn, Hodges failed to get a hit in 21 tries against the Yankees in the 1952 Series.

Lopes made 6 errors in the 1981 World Series and could have been charged with more; his misplays marred the Dodgers' win over the Yankees.

When the Tigers won pennants in 1934 and 1935, Owen hit .263 with 71 RBIs the first year and .295 with 105 RBIs the second. In the two World Series, Owen hit .069 (2-for-29) and .050 (1-for-20) and drove in only one run each October.

After he had finished among the leaders in fielding percentage and won the AL MVP in 1925, Washington's Peckinpaugh belied his reputation as a defensive whiz by making 8 errors in 40 World Series chances. Among the misplays were a dropped pop-up that allowed the Cubs to tie the score in the seventh game and a wild throw that set up the Series-winning rally.

Five years after his embarrassment in the 1980 World Series, Willie Wilson exacted his revenge by hitting .367 to help the Royals take the 1985 World Championship.

The Giants' cleanup hitter in 1911, Murray hit .291 and drove in 78 runs; in the ensuing World Series against the Athletics, he went 0-for-21.

Davis's .284 average for Los Angeles during the 1966 season dimmed when he managed only one single in 16 at-bats as the Orioles swept the Dodgers in the Series.

Wilson's .326 average, 79 stolen bases, and AL-leading totals in hits, triples, and runs scored in 1980 were all forgotten during the World Series, in which he hit a paltry .154 (4-for-26) and struck out 12 times as the Phillies bested Kansas City in 6 games.

Similarly, no one expected MVP Bench's NL highs in homers and RBIs in 1972 to translate into only one RBI, on a solo homer, in the World Series against Oakland. Even more embarrassing, Oakland reliever Rollie Fingers struck the Cincinnati slugger out in the course of what, with considerable supporting theatrics by A's manager Dick Williams, looked like an intentional pass in progress.

Frazier is the only pitcher, aside from Lefty Williams of the Black Sox, to lose 3 games in a Series; in 3 2/3 innings of relief work the righthander gave up 7 earned runs (for a 17.18 ERA).

MOMENTS IN THE SUN

Postseason play brings out the best in some players—and not just the best players.

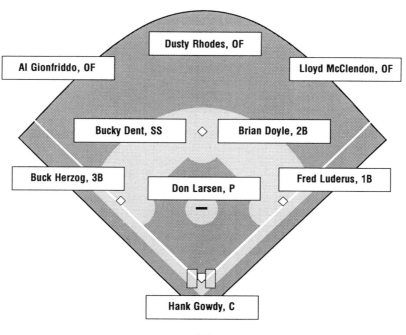

Luderus, a lifetime .277 hitter, batted .438 with a home run and 6 RBIs in his only World Series, with the 1915 Phillies.

Doyle hit a nearly invisible .161 in his four big league seasons, but replacing the injured Willie Randolph in the 1978 World Series, he hit .438, scored 4 runs, and drove in 2 more to help the Yankees defeat the Dodgers in 6 games.

To belie his .259 career average, Herzog went 12-for-30 (.400) with 4 RBIs and 6 runs scored for the Giants in the 1912 World Series.

Doyle's double-play partner Dent hit the game-winning homer that propelled the Yankees over the Red Sox in the one-game playoff for the 1978 pennant. Then he took World Series MVP honors over Doyle by hitting .417, driving in 7 runs, and scoring an additional 3; his lifetime batting average in regular-season play was only .247

The otherwise unspectacular Gionfriddo's steal of second induced Yankee manager Bucky Harris to walk the potential winning run to first intentionally just before Cookie Lavagetto broke up Bill Bevens's no-hitter in the ninth inning of the fourth game of the 1947 World Series. Gionfriddo's circus catch that set Joe DiMaggio to kicking the dirt around second base in the same Series has become part of baseball lore.

Even though he pitched the best postseason game of all time, Don Larsen never won more than 11 games during a regular season.

Rhodes hit a pinch homer to win the first game of the 1954 World Series for the Giants, blasted another one in Game 2, and batted .667 with 7 RBIs in New York's sweep of the Indians; in seven seasons, the lefty swinger hit only .253 and never accumulated more than 15 homers.

McClendon carried a career average of .244 through the 1995 season; but in the 1992 LCS he was Pittsburgh's superman, hitting .727 and slugging 1.182.

Gowdy, a career .270 hitter, led the Miracle Braves to a sweep of the mighty Athletics in 1914 by batting .545, with 5 extra-base hits.

And if you don't think Larsen was average, account some other way for his lifetime record of 81 wins and 91 losses.

THE LAST BATTER

Only sixteen postseason series—tie-breaking playoffs, LCS, or World Series—have ended with the victorious team scoring the winning run in the bottom half of the last inning of the final game. Eight of the heroes—and one goat—were:

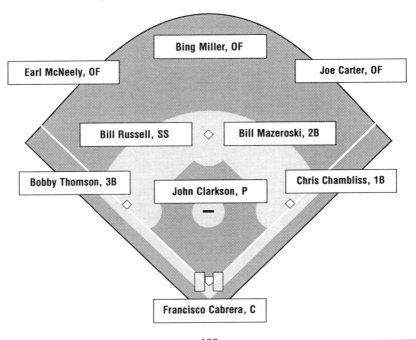

Chambliss ended the 1976 ALCS with a home run in the bottom of the ninth inning of the fifth game. With the Yankees and Royals tied at 2 games each and Kansas City having tied the final game, 6–6, in the eighth, the New York first baseman led off the ninth by sending the first pitch by righthander Mark Littell over the right-field fence to give the New Yorkers the AL pennant.

In 1960, Mazeroski concluded one of the most bizarre World Series by leading off in the ninth inning with a four-bagger that gave Pittsburgh its first world championship in thirty-five years. Although the Yankees outhit the Pirates 91–60 and outscored them 55–27, the Series came down to a seesaw seventh game in which the Pirates pulled ahead, 9–7, in the eighth with a 5-run outburst highlighted by a 3-run homer by catcher Hal Smith, only to have the Yankees tie the score in the top of the ninth. Mazeroski led off the ninth against right-hander Ralph Terry and ended matters with his sudden-death blast.

Thomson's "Shot Heard 'Round the World" was the margin of difference in a 1951 pennant race that

Bill Mazeroski

Bill Mazeroski's 1960 blast marked the only time a seven-game World Series has ended with a home run.

saw the Giants come from 13 1/2 games behind the Dodgers on August 11 to a tie at the end of the regular season. The two teams split the first two games of a best-of-three playoff series, and the Dodgers scored 3 runs in the top of the eighth to take a 4–1 lead in the finale. The Polo Grounders responded with a run in the ninth before Ralph Branca relieved Don Newcombe to face the righty slugger with runners on second and third. His first pitch to Thomson was a strike, his second was a 3-run home run that a near-hysterical Russ Hodges, the Giants' announcer could describe only by repeating "The Giants win the pennant. The Giants win the pennant. . ."

Russell's tenth-inning single to center in the fifth game of a best three-of-five NLCS gave the Dodgers the 1978 pennant by driving home Ron Cey from second base. The two-out tie-breaking RBI off southpaw reliever Tug McGraw was made possible when the usually sure-handed Garry Maddox dropped a line drive off the bat of Dusty Baker to prolong Los Angeles's turn at bat.

McNeely was credited with the Pebble Hit that ended one of the strangest sequences in postseason play and won the 1924 World Series for the Senators. With the score tied 3–3 in the bottom of the twelfth inning of the seventh game, Giants' reliever Jack Bentley got Washington catcher Muddy Ruel to hit a foul pop that looked like the second out of the inning until New York receiver Hank Gowdy tripped over his mask and dropped the ball. Ruel took advantage of the error by doubling and held second as pitcher Walter Johnson reached base on shortstop Travis Jackson's error. McNeely followed with a grounder right at third baseman Freddy Lindstrom. An anticipated double play never materialized because the ball struck a pebble and bounded over Lindstrom's head for a Series-winning RBI single. Eerily, the game reached this point only because of an almost identical play in the ninth that turned a Bucky Harris ground ball to third into a two-run game-tying base hit.

Miller was the last batter in the first postseason finale to conclude with a ninth-inning come-from-behind-victory. With the Cubs ahead by a 2–0 score in Game 5 of the 1929 Series, outfielder Mule Haas homered with one on and one out to tie the game; then, after Mickey Cochrane grounded out, Al Simmons doubled, and Jimmie Foxx was walked intentionally to get to Miller, who blasted a double off the wall to give the Athletics a world championship. The drama of the inning has been obscured because it came two days after Philadelphia had scored a record 10 runs in the seventh inning to snatch the fourth game away from Chicago by a score of 10–8.

Carter's 3-run blast in the sixth game of the 1993 Series marked the first time a World Series ended with a come-from-behind sudden-death homer. The righty slugger gave Toronto its second consecutive world championship only 2 innings after the Phillies had scored 5 runs to take a 6-5 lead. Carter's victim was lefty reliever Mitch Williams.

Third-string catcher Cabrera's pinch-hit single brought home the game-tying and pennant-winning runs for the Braves in the 1992 NLCS—the only time a championship series has ended with a home team overcoming a 2-run deficit during its final at-bat of a rubber game. Cabrera delivered against reliever Stan Belinda with the bases loaded and one run already in as Atlanta won the seventh game by a score of 3–2.

St. Louis outfielder Curt Welch has been credited with stealing home in the bottom of the tenth inning of the sixth game of an 1886 championship series between the AA Browns and the NL Cubs. Actually, Chicago righthander Clarkson uncorked a wild pitch—possibly on a pitchout—that, depending upon the contemporary version, either glanced off catcher King Kelly's glove or sailed over his head. Welch's fabled $15,000 Slide, if it took place at all, was entirely superfluous.

Honorable mention to:

Third baseman Larry Gardner, whose sacrifice fly drove in the championship run for the Red Sox in the eighth game of the 1912 Series after Boston had tied the score in a rally that included a muffed fly ball by Giants' center fielder Fred Snodgrass and a foul pop that dropped untouched next to first baseman Fred Merkle.

Outfielder Goose Goslin, who broke a sixth game 3–3 tie by driving home Mickey Cochrane with a two-out single in the bottom of the ninth that gave the Tigers their first world championship, in 1935.

Second baseman Billy Martin, who singled home the winning run in the sixth and final game of the 1953 World Series with his record twelfth hit after Brooklyn's Carl Furillo had tied the score at 3–3 with a 2-run homer in the top of the ninth.

Outfielder Ken Griffey put the finishing touch on the Reds' 3-game sweep of the Phillies in the 1976 LCS when he singled off first baseman Bobby Tolan's glove to drive in Dave Concepción after George Foster and Johnny Bench had hit back-to-back homers to tie the game 3–3.

Pinch hitter Gene Larkin, who concluded the 1991 World Series with a tenth-inning bases-loaded single that gave Jack Morris and the Twins a 1–0 victory over the Braves in Game Seven.

And extra goat horns to Pittsburgh righthanders John Miljus and Bob Moose, whose wild pitches sent home, respectively, Earle Combs (with the run that gave the Yankees a 1927 World Series sweep) and George Foster (with the tally that decided the seventh game of the 1972 NLCS in favor of the Reds).

PICTURE CREDITS

Photos:

Compliments of the Atlanta Braves: Hank Aaron.

Compliments of the Cincinnati Reds: Sparky Anderson, Ken Griffey, Ray Knight, and Pete Rose.

Compliments of the Kansas City Royals: Jackie Hernandez, Freddie Patek, George Brett, and Willie Wilson.

Compliments of the Montreal Expos: Coco Laboy.

Compliments of the New York Mets: Dave Kingman and Ed Kranepool.

Compliments of the New York Yankees: Darryl Strawberry.

Compliments of the Pittsburgh Pirates: Willie Stargell, Roberto Clemente, Kiki Cuyler, Ralph Kiner, Lloyd McClendon, and Bill Mazeroski.

Compliments of the San Diego Padres: Enzo Hernandez and Mike Ivie.

Compliments of the San Francisco Giants: Willie McCovey and Darren Lewis.

Compliments of The National Baseball Library and Archive: George Wright, John Paciorek, and Ron Necciai.

From the authors' private collection: George Kell.

Baseball Cards:

Copyright The Topps Company, Inc.: Andy Messersmith, Rick Monday, Jason Thompson, Reggie Jackson, Early Wynn, Randy Bass, Rob Deer, Mark Portugal, Tony Solaita, Vida Blue, Joe Morgan, Bobby Richardson, and Don Larsen (from the collection of Bart Acocella.); Ed Brinkman and Terry Felton (from the collection of Mark Moyer).

Reprinted with permission of Megacards, Inc., Fairfield, Iowa 52556 and The Sporting News Publishing Company, St. Louis, Missouri 63116: Babe Ruth, Luke Appling, Joe Sewell, Hal Newhouser, Charlie Gehringer, Heinie Zimmerman, Nap Lajoie, George Watkins, Hal Chase, Arlie Latham, Babe Herman, Jimmy Lavender, Max Bishop, Tony Cuccinello, Billy Herman, Arndt Jorgens, Bobby Doerr, Tris Speaker, Jackie Hayes, Pepper Martin, Honus Wagner, and Travis Jackson. (From *The Sporting News* R Conlon Collection TM.)

From the authors' private collection: Joe Jackson, Roy Campanella, Ty Cobb, Sam Crawford, Robin Roberts, Frankie Frisch, John McGraw, and Hank Greenberg.